Praise for

CONTEMPLATE: TOWARD AN EXPANSIVE HEART

"Drawing on a thorough knowledge of the literature on contemplation, his personal experience, and teaching skills, Jacob Riyeff has written an engaging and alluring introduction to what contemplation is, why we need it, and how to go about doing it. His use of the soul as a key idea, his suggestion that contemplation of other living creatures is particularly helpful in today's culture, and his incisive critique of living digitally all enrich the book." —**Fr. Hugh Feiss, OSB**, monk of Monastery of the Ascension in Jerome, Idaho and scholar of medieval monasticism

"Jacob Riyeff steps out from behind his great gifts as editor and translator to bring his poetic sensibilities to prose in this delightful collection. He is one of those lay people whose erudition about the spiritual life and history of monasticism and the contemplative tradition is the envy of many professed religious. A very welcome addition to the literature on the praxis of prayer and meditation." —**Cyprian Consiglio, OSB Cam**, *Prayer in the Cave of the Heart* and *Rediscovering the Divine*; Secretary General for Monastic Interreligious Dialogue, Rome

"Jacob Riyeff's *Contemplate* is a welcome exploration of the past, present, and possible future of the contemplative tradition in Western culture. There is much to ponder here!" —**Sr. Sarah Schwartzberg, OSB**, editor, *Spirit & Life*

This book is first in a new series, **Beyond Our Instincts***: succinct, multi-disciplinary, countercultural stances in an environment that sells us the idea that happiness is whatever we want now. These authors—all scholars of religion who are also religiously involved—suggest there are more important things, including some we may have forgotten.*

Coming in future publishing seasons:

Join *(on being together)*
Imagine *(on opting out of technique-obsessed culture)*
Wait *(on the lost value of open questions and not-knowing)*

[BEYOND OUR INSTINCTS I]

CONTEMPLATE

TOWARD AN EXPANSIVE HEART

JACOB RIYEFF

BOOK PUBLISHING COMPANY
RHINEBECK, NEW YORK

Paperback ISBN 9781966608011
eBook ISBN 9781966608028

Library of Congress Cataloging-in-Publication Data

Names: Riyeff, Jacob, 1982- author
Title: Contemplate : toward an expansive heart / Jacob Riyeff.
Description: Rhinebeck, New York : Monkfish Book Publishing Company, [2025] | Series: Beyond our instincts ; 1 | Includes bibliographical references.
Identifiers: LCCN 2025026988 (print) | LCCN 2025026989 (ebook) | ISBN 9781966608011 paperback | ISBN 9781966608028 ebook
Subjects: LCSH: Contemplation
Classification: LCC BV5091.C7 R59 2025 (print) | LCC BV5091.C7 (ebook) | DDC 248.3/4--dc23/eng/20250828
LC record available at https://lccn.loc.gov/2025026988
LC ebook record available at https://lccn.loc.gov/2025026989

Book and cover design by Colin Rolfe

Monkfish Book Publishing Company
22 East Market Street, Suite 304
Rhinebeck, New York 12572
(845) 876-4861
monkfishpublishing.com

With all watchfulness keep thy heart,
because life issueth out from it.

Proverbs 4:23

To be contemplative as Christ is contemplative is to be open to all the fullness that the Father wishes to pour into our hearts. With our minds made still and ready to receive, with our self-generated fantasies about God and ourselves reduced to silence, we are at last at the point where we may begin to grow. And the face we need to show to our world is the face of a humanity in endless growth towards love, a humanity so delighted and engaged by the glory of what we look towards that we are prepared to embark on a journey without end to find our way more deeply into it, into the heart of the trinitarian life....

And we seek this not because we are in search of some private 'religious experience' that will make us feel secure or holy. We seek it because in this self-forgetting gazing towards the light of God in Christ we learn how to look at one another and at the whole of God's creation....

In this perspective, contemplation is very far from being just one kind of thing that Christians do: it is the key to prayer, liturgy, art and ethics, the key to the essence of a renewed humanity that is capable of seeing the world and other subjects in the world with freedom – freedom from self-oriented, acquisitive habits and the distorted understanding that comes from them. To put it boldly, contemplation is the only ultimate answer to the unreal and insane world that our financial systems and our advertising culture and our chaotic and unexamined emotions encourage us to inhabit. To learn contemplative practice is to learn what we need so as to live truthfully and honestly and lovingly. It is a deeply revolutionary matter.

Archbishop Rowan Williams,
Address to an assembly of Catholic bishops in Rome

CONTENTS

IV. CONTEMPLATION IN THE WORLD

V. LOOKING FORWARD

INTRODUCTION

For all that they enjoy the familiar, the human mind and body tend to long for novelty too: internal chatter and new sense stimuli and satisfactions that they both get to share. And this seems to have been the case all along, not a unique quality of the modern world. Yet modernity, especially our unprecedented consumer economies and digital worlds, offers us new avenues for this incessant focus on the next thing, the next momentary fulfillment.

This may not be terrible, if we find human life to be primarily an empty container to "fill up" with things and experiences to temporarily placate our desires until the next one comes along, before the unthinkable dissolution of death.

But the religious traditions of the world have all taught that there is much more to human life than this, that in fact the endless chatter in our minds (and on our tongues), and the gratification of our sensual desires, are, when left unchecked, opposed to what's ultimately valuable in human life. When asked what the purpose of human life is, the ancient Greek philosopher Anaxagoras answered: "to contemplate all the various creatures" (*eis theorian*). In as much as the chatter and sense gratification gets in the way of that, they're harmful to human flourishing.

The early western Christian tradition was no different. Modern Benedictine Dom Cuthbert Butler says, "It was the standard teaching in the Catholic ages down to modern times that contemplation is the natural term of a spiritual life seriously lived, and is a thing to be desired, aspired to, aimed at, and not infrequently attained to by devout souls."[1] For the ancient and medieval Church, the need to discipline the body and the mind was not primarily a moral issue (moral adherence was assumed) but a means to the clear vision of heavenly realities in contemplation—a kind of spiritual "seeing" in the soul—a polishing of the glass of the inner eye. That traditional view of who we are has been obscured for a long while. But we can reclaim this view, this practice. That's what this book is trying to say something about.

As in my own life for the last two decades, in this book I turn to the western contemplative tradition to ask, *How can we live a contemplative life today, in this particular society and culture? How can we live a more grounded life, one open to the Spirit? One in which our hearts are ever expanding in charity to reach out to our human neighbors, other creatures, the earth, and the Source and Foundation of all that is, which we usually call "God"?*[2] I listen to the answers that western contemplatives have offered for the last sixteen-hundred years or so, and share what I've learned. I hope and pray it might open some space in your heart as well.

---

[1] Cuthbert Butler, *Western Mysticism* (Grey Arrow, 1960), 190.

[2] As a member of the Catholic communion myself, when I hear the word "God," I tend to want to replace it with "Trinity," since the communion of three divine Persons in the one divine Substance is foundational to my own understanding in faith of what the word "God" refers to—and this understanding is the lens through which I see everything else in life. However, I realize and hope that plenty of people who read this book may not be Trinitarian Christians, so I will mostly employ words like "God" and "Creator" throughout. (A couple times I will have something to say specifically to my Trinitarian comrades, which I hope can still be of interest to anyone else reading.) One last note in this context: let us recall that even the word "God" (which we often take to be a kind of generic word for the divine being) is also a kind of title that refers to the Source and Foundation of all that is in a particular way. Fourteenth-century Eastern monk St. Gregory Palamas, who will turn up a few times here, explains in his discussion of the divine essence and energies: "Likewise the term God (*Theos*) we have taken from His providential and overseeing activity. In this manner, then, by the term God we have been taught about a certain partial activity of the divine nature, but we have not attained an understanding of God's essence by this word" (St. Gregory Palamas, "Topics of Natural and Theological Science and on the Moral and Ascetic Life: One Hundred and Fifty Texts" in *The Philokalia: The Complete Text,* trans. G.E.H. Palmer, Phillip Sherrard, and Kallistos Ware (Faber and Faber, 1995), IV.385-86). *Caveat lector.*

A BRIEF (AND SOMEWHAT CHEEKY) SKETCH OF CONTEMPLATION IN WESTERN HISTORY

For those who might like a general timeline of the main contours of the contemplative tradition in the west, here is a brief sketch. (See much more detail in the sources listed in "Works Referenced.") Those who don't feel such a need should feel free to skip this brief chapter.

One note on "the west": it is a fraught term. But here it serves as a shorthand for the sociocultural zone of those peoples who for many centuries were affected by Greek thought but mainly lived in the political orbit of the western Roman Empire and the religious orbit of the bishop of Rome (the pope). This is more or less continuous with the societies that gave us (for better and worse) the Scientific Revolution, the Enlightenment, and the Industrial Revolution. There was of course lots else going on in the west itself, in Eastern Christianity, and in other religious traditions. But these chapters primarily wrestle with and draw inspiration from the west's contemplative tradition from St. John Cassian through Dame Gertrude More, with a couple of more modern voices mixed in. You've been warned.

Ca. 600-300 BCE: Early Greek philosophers started questioning and thinking about the world in systematic ways. They saw contemplation as key to a happy human life. Athenagoras went so far as to say that our primary purpose in life is "to behold" the world. Plato and Aristotle said stuff too.

Ca. 1000-400 BCE: The Hebrew prophets started having visions of God and angels, and they received revelations. They started meditating on all this and wrote inspired books filled with wisdom, political commentary, and much else besides.

Ca. 0: On the Trinitarian reading, the second Person of the Trinity, co-eternal image of the Father, becomes incarnate to redeem humanity and reconcile everything in heaven and on earth, inviting us back into Trinitarian life through his Resurrection and sending forth of the Holy Spirit.

Ca. 45-100: St. Paul is rapt to the "third heaven," writes lots of letters; St. John contemplates the Word and God-as-Love.

Ca. 250-275: Plotinus devises a whole system of contemplation based in a contemplative reunion of the individual with "the One."

Ca. 250-350: The Desert Fathers and Mothers flee to their deserts. They start chanting the psalms and living alone in silence, engaging in what St. John Cassian calls "fiery prayer" in purity of heart.

Throughout 4th Century: The Roman Empire legalizes Christianity, monks gather in more places, monasteries become seeds of what will become known as "the contemplative life." They shepherd contemplation as a "lifting up of the soul" to divine things and divine Light for several centuries.

Ca. 1200: New learning comes into Europe, which sets in motion a clearer division between those who privilege contemplation (who will eventually be called "mystics") and those who privilege study (who will eventually become what we think of as "academics"). The categorizing and labelling of different contemplative states begins and continues for several centuries, drawing on more eastern models, especially that of a Syrian monk now called Pseudo-Dionysius.

Ca. 1500-1700: Contemplation becomes more and more thought of as "mysticism"—exceptional experiences of divine union, visions, etc. A movement called "Quietism" becomes a problem, but mainly because science and the Enlightenment have become different kinds of problems.

Ca. 1800-present day: With the modern era's exultation of instrumental reason and the machine, contemplation becomes seen more and more either as the relatively useless thing academics and poets do, or the mystical thing religious zealots do. The west forgets the contemplative tradition or sees it as a backward, “medieval” thing that good, rational consumers don’t mess about with.

20th Century: Amidst the emergence of New Age spirituality, the bohemian and hippie countercultures, and the mainstream discovery of Far Eastern religions, some folks, mainly monastics, start reclaiming and making widely available again the western contemplative tradition, though it remains unknown to many and conflated with the earlier mentioned movements by others.

Today: Here we are. Will we embrace the contemplative path and long for hearts expanded by deep intimacy with reality and our Creator’s indwelling, gratuitous, unfailing love?

WE HAVE A CONTEMPLATION PROBLEM

We are speaking of an attitude of the heart, one which approaches life with serene attentiveness, which is capable of being fully present to someone without thinking of what comes next, which accepts each moment as a gift from God to be lived to the full. Jesus taught us this attitude when he invited us to contemplate the lilies of the field and the birds of the air, or when seeing the rich young man and knowing his restlessness, "he looked at him with love" (Mk. 10:21).
Pope Francis, *Laudato Si'* §226

There is a stillness of the human person, body and soul. In that stillness we rest in the intuition of our existing, our existing along with other creatures. In that stillness too, God is sometimes seen in the foundation of the soul—as much as that is possible for a creature in this limited life.

Such is the promise held out by the contemplative tradition of the Church. Contemplation lost its prominent place in western Christian spirituality throughout the eighteenth century for a host of reasons we'll touch on throughout this work, but it lives on. It persists in clear and insightful moments in prayer, on a walk along a river, or in the gaze at a small child engaging the world anew. Its more dramatic, "higher" stages (ecstasy, "glimpsing the divine light," etc.) are still found in quiet rooms and monastery walls. But, also, for so many Christians, contemplation is not even on their radars, maybe it's even dangerous. At the intersection of our economic, socio-cultural, political, and religious lives, we have a contemplation problem.

What is contemplation? It is a direct beholding. A direct beholding of what? Tradition holds that there is natural contemplation and contemplation specifically supported by grace. There is a natural contemplation of creatures, an aesthetic contemplation of art, a spiritual contemplation of heavenly realities and divinity itself. The dividing line between what's a purely creaturely capacity for contemplation and what's a graced or supernatural contemplation is admittedly somewhat murky. (The systems that developed to make stark distinctions between all the "levels" of contemplation, for all their value, generally end up feeling unhooked from actual experience, so I won't be following any of them closely here.) What is common to all forms of contemplation is the simplicity of direct intuition, a gathering of the whole person in recognition of what is present. Sometimes this includes loss of body consciousness and rapture. For most of us, contemplation of whatever sort will be quieter, less dramatic, yet not necessarily any less profound.

Our primary contemplation problem is that our mechanized day-to-day activities shape our inner and outer worlds, our consciousness and our activity, in ways that work against contemplative awareness. The broader historical and social background to all this, alluded to above—the fact that the Catholic reaction to the Reformation, that the Scientific Revolution, that the Enlightenment, that the Industrial Revolution all disrupted the Church's contemplative tradition in the west—is a long and winding story. But, as inheritors of all this history that we cannot change, we can opt to focus on more concrete aspects of the problem that perhaps we can change.

As a cottage industry of culture critics have been pointing out for some time, with the advent of industrial civilization, the advance of machines into so much of our individual and collective lives, mass media, and now the proliferation of the internet, the smartphone, and machine learning, we in the modern west are habituated to mechanical living. We adapt our daily activities, our bodies' movements, to our machines. We look at what our machines proffer to our gaze. We reorganize our economies and the earth itself for our machines. We value efficiency in and of itself because it feeds our desire for more and more efficient machines. In all this, we are conditioned to behold not reality directly but the mediations of all manner of machines, screens, and devices.

And no: this is not another screed about how we're all distracted. Rather, a substantial part of our contemplation problem is precisely that we're not distracted at all. We're very much attentive, deeply focused on a variety of machines and mediations of words, concepts, visuals, and sounds. A contemplative master of the twelfth century, Richard of St. Victor, aptly noted that "Where love is, there is the eye."[1] That is, by discerning where our attention and affection are directed, we find what we genuinely care about. Our claims of concern for this person or that movement, our cultivation of virtue or our desire for God must stand amidst the evidence of where we give our attention, our physical eyes and the "eye" of our consciousness day in and day out.

This is one crucial aspect of the contemplation problem particular to our era. We can devotedly attend to things that feel so important, when we are really—or, at least, also always—attending to a machine. A machine that was almost surely made with components from open-pit mines gathered by people with deplorable working conditions, made by extractive and exploitative companies, and that relies on the continued support of those companies and the burning of fossil fuels. A machine that is an integral part of a system of predatory global capitalism. I'm using one now as I type this, because no publisher today would accept a handwritten manuscript, given our economic systems.

Another aspect of this contemplation problem particular to our digitally-saturated lives has to do with the discursive intensity

---

[1] Richard of St. Victor, *The Twelve Patriarchs: Benjamin Minor* in *Twelve Patriarchs, The Mystical Ark, and Book Three of The Trinity* (Paulist Press, 1979), XIII, 65.

of so much of the internet and televisual media. Contemplation is a function of the intuition, simple awareness, the direct beholding and apprehension of a given object of consciousness, from lichen to the divine substance.

The more concepts, words, and ideas there are floating around in our consciousness, and the more emotional reactions (not necessarily responses) we have to all this, the more we cover over and obscure the simplicity and immediacy of contemplation. In the "always on" life filled with checking in on the smartphone while we wait in lines, sit on the bus, walk down the hall, sit and watch TV with our families at night, the intellect and reason (not to mention the imagination and senses) have continual grist for their mills, denying intuition and simple awareness space in the playing field of consciousness.

This is not to say there's anything wrong with words or arguments or emotions. But when we regularly refuse to look away from such discursive intensity, when we habitually immerse our minds and bodies in this seemingly unending sprawl of the next thing, we train our consciousness in mediation and notion, depriving the mind and heart of the possibility for, an habitual openness to, direct encounter with reality. This point perhaps assumes fresh poignancy in the face of the relatively new wave of generative software, machines making novel but always-derivative discourse and images and audio at our whim.

A more extreme example can perhaps drive to the heart of this contemplation problem. This is the pervasive and much-lamented problem that an easy internet has proliferated and made readily accessibile: pornography. Though contemplation and pornography are not usually discussed together, the arresting of attention that occurs when one beholds a naked human form is, I argue, a contemplative response. Who has not been awed by the beauty of Michelangelo's *David*? Or—if one has seen the less famous statue—Lorenzo Bartolini's *The Woman and the Serpent*? Human bodies are parts of the natural world. When we view a naked human body, our inner discourse, our words and concepts, tend to halt for a span of time in response to the radical vulnerability of another. The discursive mind pauses and we shift to an intuitive response, simply beholding. (This response is likely more intense for us due to how little we see other people's bodies directly and in person.) But then, in the case of pornography, we usually move on to other business, which is not so lofty but still outside the domain of the discursive. Pornography takes what can and *should* be an appreciative contemplative response (natural and aesthetic), or even an invitation to direct interpersonal communion (spiritual), and frustrates that possibility by its very nature. Because the other person isn't actually present: the potential interpersonal encounter is reduced to a media experience of humans removed from one another in time and space, and so the encounter turns one back on oneself, a self-oriented experience of self-satisfaction instead of an interpersonal experience of mutual contemplation, mutual satisfaction, and mutual self-giving. This is problematic in a particular way in the Trinitarian understanding of God and our creation in the image and likeness of that Trinitarian communion. If we are creatures made foundationally *in relationship* with others (in the image and likeness of the three divine Persons who empty themselves eternally into one another), our turning our sexuality back upon ourselves is a frustration of the very structure of our being.

Though pornography is an extreme example of the perversion of the intrinsic human capacity for contemplation, more pedestrian online encounters have a similar structure—seeing pictures of a dog or a flower on the internet also does not allow for an actual creaturely interaction and direct encounter, always removing the *im-* from immediacy. As with words, there's nothing intrinsically wrong with a picture, but when we absent-mindedly take the representation for the thing itself and build a life on this equivocation, we get into shakier territory.

We are creatures made for beholding, creation made conscious of itself. We have the capacity for wonder, for a kind or degree of self-aware giving of ourselves that other creatures don't seem capable of. We have supernatural gifts of faith, hope, and charity. And we give the lion's share of our spare conscious moments to non-living objects, the works of our hands, mediations, while the world suffers. We satisfy our desire for stimulation, reaction, and novelty.

We train ourselves to think and emote endlessly but not to *stop* and *see* that the moment we are in will never occur again. That the creatures we share these moments with are each unique gifts to the world from the Father through the Son in the Spirit.

As Josef Pieper tenderly reminds us, even mundane experiences like looking in a child's face can suddenly erupt into intuitive, non-rational recognitions "that the world is plumb and sound, that everything comes to its appointed goal; that in spite of all appearances, underlying all things is—peace, salvation, *gloria*; that nothing and no one is lost."[2] In daily training ourselves for deep (or scattered but forceful) focus on the next thing, on endless discursive noise, on mediation, we're missing it.

We have a contemplation problem.

[2] Josef Pieper, *Happiness and Contemplation* (Pantheon, 1958), 84.

ON THE HEART AND ITS STIFLING

The lamp of the body is the eye. If your eye is sound, your whole body will be filled with light; but if your eye is bad, your whole body will be in darkness. And if the light in you is darkness, how great will the darkness be.
Matt. 6:22-23

There is a sentimental and saccharine association with "the heart" in modern culture. There are red and pink Valentine's Day hearts on everything for a month or so a year, candies and chocolates. There are emoji hearts and email reaction hearts. While all this heart stuff in our culture can be seen as a crass cheapening of the deepest affections we have for other people, I think the continued popularity of the heart as a symbol suggests for many a real desire to convey and make tangible those stirrings within of a desire to go out of themselves, to will others' happiness, to express a longing to share life with others.[1]

This book is subtitled "Toward an Expansive Heart" for two reasons. First, St. Benedict, the founding figure of western monasticism, says in his sixth-century Rule that the monastic life, while "bound to be narrow at the outset," will lead us to a life in which "we shall run on

[1] I had finished this book before Pope Francis's encyclical letter on the Sacred Heart of Jesus, *Dilexit nos*, appeared. I can't recommend that document enough.

the path of God's commandments, our hearts overflowing with the inexpressible delight of love."[2] The phrase translated here as "our hearts overflowing" is *dilatato corde* in Benedict's Latin—"with heart expanding or widening." The rigors, deprivations, and austerities associated with the monastic life (and the contemplative life more generally) are not intended to constrict life, despite appearances and the assumptions of folks who understand freedom as mainly doing whatever one's whim is at any given time. Rather, the channeling of energy, affection, and life itself through discipline is intended to "open" the heart up, make some room within us to extend our awareness and our charity out to the world and ultimately to our Creator. (Or, rather, to our Creator and so out into the world.) So Dame Gertrude More, Benedict's seventeenth-century disciple living in exile from her native England, prayed in her personal "confession": "I beseech thee enlarge my heart and soul in longing and sighing after thee, my only beloved."[3]

Though the word "heart" (in Hebrew, Greek, and Latin) in the Hebrew Scriptures does refer to the physical organ, it also refers more commonly to the seat of one's whole inner life. The emotions, yes, but also the will and the intellect and the reason—all of it. So the heart signifies the spirit, but still the physical organ too. It's a slippery term, and seems to refer to the most intimate and life-giving aspects of who we are.[4] St. Gregory the Great, the sixth-century pope, monk, and author of the *Life of St. Benedict*, commenting on Job 7:13, says:

> In Holy Scripture, bed, bunk, or couch is often understood as the secret place of the heart. That is why the bride in the Song of Songs, who typifies each individual soul when she is moved to holy love by hidden urgings, says, *In my bed at night I sought the one*

[2] Benedict of Nursia, *The Rule of St. Benedict* (Liturgical Press, 1981), Prol:48-49.
[3] Dame Gertrude More, *Confessions of a Lover*, Confession 6, my own working edition based on the sole extant manuscript.
[4] See *The New Catholic Encyclopedia* s.v. "Heart (in the Bible)" and "Sacred Heart, Devotion to."

> *my soul loves* (Song 3:1). The beloved is unquestionably sought at night and in bed, because the invisible form of the Creator, when every image of bodily sight has been put aside, is surely found on the couch of the heart. That is why Truth says to these same lovers of his, *The kingdom of God is within you* (Lk. 17:21).[5]

The heart is the secret place of our personhood embracing physical and spiritual dimensions of our existence, the seat of life, the source of our acts and of our communion with others and with God in the most direct fashion.

The "contemplation problem" I sketched in the last chapter bears directly on this notion of the heart, and vice versa. How does the kind of life we are encouraged to live in late-modern, neoliberal, digital consumer capitalism affect and shape our hearts? That is where we have to start from if we are going to see clearly how to begin to embrace more and more a contemplative life oriented toward the expansion or dilation of the heart. And this not in a sentimental way but in the most practical, existential, sometimes gut-wrenching, always achingly beautiful ways.

For this form of life we are given by our societies now, as many of us realize even if we don't want to say it out loud, straitens our hearts, narrows them, and callouses them over so that it can be difficult to remain open and vulnerable to all that being alive in the Creator's world has to offer us, even to *want* to remain open and vulnerable.

The twentieth-century French philosopher Gabriel Marcel can help us see why this is the case. Marcel faced head-on the situation of the human person in the modern world built upon "technique," which he defines as "a specialized and rationally elaborated form of knowledge," which may end up looking like a machine but also includes processes and systems.[6] Though our rational and technological pursuits have provided some spectacular results (e.g., when my wife's lung spontaneously collapsed earlier in the year I was finishing

[5] Gregory the Great, *Moral Reflections on the Book of Job*, VIII.XXIV.41, 186-87.
[6] Gabriel Marcel, *The Decline of Wisdom* (Harvill, 1954), 7.

this book, nurses, hospital staff, and her surgeon were able to ensure that the injury did not debilitate her for life or kill her), letting the positives justify shaping practically all of our systems and even our social and recreational lives around efficiency, productivity, profit, and industrial systems has wrought sad and painful results. Why? Marcel tells us that "every kind of technical progress [entails], for the individual who takes advantage of it *without having had any share in the effort at overcoming difficulties of which such a progress is the culmination*, the payment of a heavy price, of which a certain degradation at the spiritual level is the natural expression." While "every kind of outward technical progress ought to be balanced in man by an effort at inner conquest, directed towards an ever greater self-mastery"—"it may be said that the more a man becomes dependent on the gadgets whose smooth functioning assures him a tolerable life at the material level, the more estranged he becomes from an awareness of his inner reality. I should be tempted to say that the center of gravity of such a man and his balancing point tend to become external to himself."[7] The heart is dispersed in our frantic activity and nigh-constant training of our awareness outward in heavily directed ways.

And then, as if he saw our smartphone-, augmented reality-, "artificial intelligence"-saturated situation in a crystal ball, he sums up the spiritual problem this way: "[The person dependent on his gadgets] projects himself more and more into objects, into the various pieces of apparatus on which he depends for his existence. It would be no exaggeration to say that the more progress 'humanity' as an abstraction makes towards the mastery of nature, the more actual individual men tend to become slaves of this very conquest."[8] The more taken up we become with external "technical apparatus," the more difficult it is to be aware of and sensitive to, let alone discipline in order to let flower, the inner life of the spirit. In becoming dependent upon technique, we slowly externalize our perception of ourselves and attach

[7] Gabriel Marcel, *Man against Mass Society* (Henry Regnery, 1952), 40, 41.
[8] Marcel, *Man against Mass Society*, 44.

ourselves to machinery rather than to other living creatures and the earth itself. "Life, as it were, tends to shrink back on itself, to wither."

Without arguing that we ought to retreat from all technology or from society—as this isn't really possible at this point anyhow—what is to be done? How to reorient daily living and start to cultivate the heart toward its expansion? Marcel actually says it implicitly in what he claims our civilization particularly leaves out: "A civilization in which technical progress is tending to emancipate itself more and more from speculative knowledge, a civilization in which, one may say, finally denies the place of contemplation and shuts out the possibility of contemplation, such a civilization, I say, sets us inevitably on the road toward a philosophy which is not so much a *love of wisdom* as a *hatred of wisdom*."[9] It is the denial of a place to contemplation that quietly characterizes our civilization. The drive to control; to ceaselessly take up the attention with more media, more information, more content, more problems to solve; the drive to see life itself as little more than "information processing" and "problem solving"—this civilizational drive is one that directs us away from contemplation, that frustrates our natural (and supernatural) capacity for contemplation. To the point that many people don't even know what contemplation, natural or religious, is. To them, the inner life is a mystery, let alone the yoking of inner and outer lives in a harmony that is the real flowering of spiritual life.

In a world obsessed with technique, with mastery over nature, with letting systems and tools dominate and obscure life, we tend away from self-discipline, from reflection on our inner and outer lives as *lives*, and we train ourselves not to cope with all those aspects of life that technique simply cannot help with—loss, peace, wisdom, and finally and most importantly, death. Technique has nothing to contribute to these, and if we devote our lives to rational mastery, we will neglect to prepare ourselves for these very creaturely, living realities. Technique prepares us for *control*, not for *life*.

---

[9] Marcel, *Man against Mass Society*, 44.

What is the pivot needed, if this technique-centric training of the human person is as dangerous as Marcel (and plenty of others) claim? He calls the needed disposition "a kind of inner grip that is nothing other than an ingatheredness...a kind of concentration and, as it were, inner reflection." To reject an "inhuman future" and a present-day of the same, "it is through ingatheredness only, through recollection in the highest sense of that word, though a concentrated recalling of ourselves to ourselves, that those powers of love and humility can be born."[10] This can lead us back to the direct encounter with life, to contemplation, and, hopefully, to wisdom. To an expansion of the heart.

[10] Marcel, *Man against Mass Society*, 68, 75.

THE BODY CANNOT, WILL NOT BE DENIED: ON THE BODY IN CONTEMPLATION

O God, you are my God—
it is you I seek!
For you my body yearns;
for you my soul thirsts…
Ps. 63:2

If you're feeling like what I described in the last chapters as a "contemplation problem" is explaining something you've not been able to put your finger on, or if you're simply wondering about the Church's contemplative tradition, I'd like to share what I've gleaned from my literary, scholarly, and spiritual immersion in that tradition over the last two decades. And a good place to start—as conversations with students, parishioners, and seekers in the wilderness have shown me again and again—is to get a handle on *who* and *what* we are as human creatures first.

The ancient and medieval ways of understanding who and what we are as human creatures do not fit neatly in with what our industrially-shaped, digitally-saturated lives condition us to understand ourselves as. So, thinking about prayer and contemplation with people from long ago can seem like we're "talking past each other" a lot of the time. In those conversations I mentioned above, time and again I've found that we simply don't see what a human being *is* in the same way anymore, what the body and the soul *are* in the same way anymore. But if we pray and contemplate with our bodies and souls, we need to have a handle on *them* before we dive into contemplation itself—or we'll constantly find ourselves on shifting sands, not really seeing that the life of prayer, the contemplative life is always *practical.* So first, let's talk about the body. Rather, *our bodies.*

As I start relating how the late-antique and medieval thinkers understood who and what we are, would you do me a favor? After reading this paragraph, would you please take a moment, a good solid moment, and turn your attention to your body? Nothing to evaluate, nothing to optimize, nothing to *do* beyond becoming firmly aware of what your body is like right now. Turn your awareness to the muscle inside your forearm. Or feel deeply into the side of your knee with your attention. What is it like to turn your awareness to the inside of your abdominal cavity? Where you imagine your liver is? Hold your attention there for a while and simply linger there.

Back? Wait—you didn't actually do it? Please? Okay, back for real? Cool.

Our bodies are mysteries. By the way, they are decidedly *not* machines; they/we are organisms: self-ordering, organically growing, spontaneously living individual biological organisms. If you think biology has us figured out, take a look at biologist Stephen Talbott's essay "The Unbearable Wholeness of Beings." What makes something alive different from something dead or not-alive is, at root, still a complete mystery to us on an empirical level. Despite the fact that we can empirically observe them relatively well, in some ways our bodies are more mysterious than our souls. Isaac of Stella, a twelfth-century Cistercian abbot, once said that he knows little about God, less about the soul, and still less about the body. For the body is "dark," meaning not open to the clear light of understanding.[1]

Very early, the Church recognized what the ancients generally

[1] Isaac of Stella, "The Letter of Isaac of Stella on the Soul," in *Three Treatises on Man* (Cistercian Publications, 1977), 155-77 at 155-56.

recognized: the human person is not just some matter moving around, nor are we pure spirits. The human person is a bodily principle and a spiritual principle *together*. Early apologists like St. Irenaeus and Athenagoras built whole treatises on the notion that humans are not only souls but fundamentally bodies as well. St. Irenaeus says in his *Against Heresies*: "That we, however, are a body taken from the earth and a soul that receives the Spirit of God, everyone will acknowledge,"[2] noting nonchalantly how his audience would agree with this basic notion of what a human person is. Many of the early heresies, on the other hand, either denied that Christ had a real body, that our bodies mattered in the end, or both. The Church worked tirelessly to make clear that both body and soul matter, that we are what I'll call a body+soul. If we are the kind of creature that contemplates, we do that contemplating as a body+soul.

It's true that, due to different factors, like the martyrs' disregard for their bodily lives and some early fathers' drawing on pagan philosophers, a certain devaluation of the body has plagued some Christian spiritual thinkers and moralists down the centuries. But the steady and firm teaching of the Church couldn't be clearer: "Do you not know that your body is a temple of the Holy Spirit within you…? Therefore, glorify God in your body," St. Paul tells the Corinthians (1 Cor. 6:19-20). He also assures us that "when this which is corruptible clothes itself with incorruptibility and this which is mortal clothes itself with immortality, then the word that is written shall come about: 'Death is swallowed up in victory'" (1 Cor. 15:54). Not for Christians is the notion that we will all live as spirits for all eternity—no, the flesh will rise again from its humiliation and decay, standing firm and seeing the divine light bodily for all eternity! Job puts it like this: "From my flesh I will see God: I will see for myself, my own eyes, not another's, will behold him" (Job 19:26-27). Even the zeal of the martyrs can readily be interpreted as not disdain for the body, but a desire to put faithfulness above all else;

[2] Irenaeus of Lyons, *Against Heresies*, in *The Ante-Nicene Fathers*, vol. 1 (William B. Eerdmans, 1967), III.22, 454.

those who venerated the martyrs were not extolling their life without a body, but celebrated those bodies in the cult of relics. Likewise, some early fathers' use of pagan philosophy that saw the body as a "prison" were difficult to square with the fully embodied and integral nature of the human person found throughout the Scriptures. When we read people like St. Augustine or St. Gregory of Nyssa carefully, we can see a very real tension surrounding how they value the soul above the body and how the Scriptures themselves speak about who we are. The psalmist cries out: "O God, you are my God—it is you I seek! For you my body yearns; for you my soul thirsts" (Ps. 63:2). Body+soul.

But let's get back to us. Would you do me another favor? Move your hand around. Open and close your palm. Run your fingers back and forth. All that moving? We don't really understand how it works, how the body *lives*. The ancient way of understanding the body's movements—*all* the body's movements—was that the soul animates the body's matter, and this is central to how I think the body matters in the contemplative life. For it's not that the soul "controls" the body like a crane operator controls a crane. Rather the soul suffuses the body wholly all the time, until death.

Very often, when I talk with students and older adults alike, I find that we have a general sense of the body not being "us." That somehow the mind, the reason, the emotions, or the soul is us, and the body is really just an instrument that we use to get around. This is the sentiment conveyed in that inspirational line that floats around online that "You are not a body. You are a soul. You *have* a body." I think I understand how that message is trying to be positive. (In a superficial, objectifying, pornographic culture like ours, it's trying to help people break free of that objectification, I suppose?) But this is completely *not* the view of the long tradition of the Church. Rather, we are very much our bodies, as we are very much our souls. We are bodies+souls together. Rather than rejecting our bodies as us, we should reject our culture's objectification and superficial evaluation of bodies outright!

So how is it different to say that the body moves due to the soul's activity? The idea that somehow my soul is really just in my head and controls my body like a machine made out of meat came more or less from a French philosopher named René Descartes (1596-1650). This "mindification" of the human was being thrown around by lots of thinkers within a hundred years of Descartes's work, lots of philosophers and writers focusing on human reason (a newly calculative human reason) as the most important thing in the world, showing how we could control the world around us if we simply used our reason. Which in some ways was a really good thing (like when we stopped killing each other because some of us gave our religious allegiance to the bishop of Rome and some did not).

But it also had some pretty dire effects on how we view ourselves and our relationships with the creatures around us and the earth itself. Add in the Scientific Revolution and the Industrial Revolution, and folks started seeing themselves more and more as something "inside" the body that used the body instrumentally to get around. The body became just another "thing" that the mind manipulated to get what it wanted, because the mind was suddenly in control and separate in a way it hadn't really been before that. But when we stop to think about it some, that's absurd. Organisms don't work like that.

There was wisdom in the old way of understanding ourselves as body+soul. And the proof of that is how unhealthy so many of us are today, physically, emotionally, socially, spiritually. We divide ourselves up, isolate ourselves from the world, other people, and other creatures, even from our own bodies (in our imaginations at least), and then wonder why folks don't seem well. Why we're "burned out." Why we feel rootless. Why we don't know what to do with the life we've been given. As former Archbishop of Canterbury Rowan Williams once said, "Being a creature is in danger of becoming a lost art."[3] The sixth-century scholar Cassiodorus affirmed that "the soul

[3] Rowan Williams, "On Being Creatures" in *On Christian Theology* (Blackwell, 2000), 63-78 at 77. I am glad to have been reading this essay on the morning of my last revision of this book before final submission, as it is very resonant

benefits from the healthy balance of the flesh, feeds on the gaze of its eyes, delights in hearing sound, enjoys the sweetest odors, and is attracted by the necessary pleasure of eating. Although the senses in no way nourish the soul, it is afflicted with the deepest sorrow if deprived of them."[4] Cassiodorus notes that this affection for the body can lead us into error, but he is also unequivocal in the delight that our souls find in our bodies. Maybe we can rediscover this delight in "the healthy balance of the flesh" as well.

A twentieth-century English Benedictine abbot, Dom Justin McCann, affirmed this long tradition in ways that pushed back against the modern view of the soul or mind as something "in" the body but not really related to it meaningfully (not to mention the materialist view that sees the human as only matter, even consciousness itself as only matter). His way of speaking about the unity of body+soul is worth quoting at length. (Throughout, I've changed his use of the word "man" to "person" with appropriate pronouns.)

> A person preserves, throughout their life, their personal identity. This identity rests, in the first place, on identity of soul. The conscious life, knit together by memory, is continuous from beginning to end, and the person themselves recognizes in this continuous experience their identity with themselves. But such *spiritual identity* is not the whole of the matter, just as a person is not a pure spirit, but a being composed of body and soul. So that there is also a psycho-physical identity, based on the life of the senses and on every vital process of the organism. Let us call this, to distinguish it from the other, *vital identity*.... We recognize, then, in a living person, not merely an identity of soul, but an identity of their

---

with what I am trying to say here, though in a more strictly theological key. I won't refashion the whole essay as it is too late in the process, but here's a piece to chew on in light of my current topic: "Hence...the importance of attention to the praying *body*; the contemplative significance of taking time to *sense* ourselves in prayer, to perceive patiently what and where we materially are" (76).

[4] Cassiodorus, *On the Soul*, in *Institutions of Divine and Secular Learning* and *On the Soul* (Liverpool University Press, 2004), ch. 4, 244.

> complete self, an identity not only in the functions of their mind, but in every function of their sensitive organism. Physiologists say that the substance of which the body is composed is continually changing.... But it is a plain fact of experience that this process, however constant and however complete, does not interrupt the vital identity. Though atoms and molecules may change, yet the unitary life persists, and the organism goes on uninterruptedly to the dissolution of death, preserving a continuous vital identity.[5]

McCann's sense of a "vital identity" seems to be lacking for many of us today. We perceive our bodies as something we have to deal with rather than an integral part of everything that we are, our vital identity. How else could we have the common experience of "losing" ourselves in a screen for hours before realizing it, let alone have prominent people in the public spotlight dream (and be taken seriously) about uploading minds to computers to "live" in computer simulations? This last used to be an extreme view, but is now somehow accepted (even if not taken terribly seriously by many) as just another thing to believe is possible rather than frightening dystopian stuff. But as another English Benedictine, Dom Anscar Vonier, has asked in a discussion of the bodily resurrection: "Has...anyone... ever known what it is to be without a body, without bodily life? What are we doing, when we become idealists, but projecting into eternity the experience of bodily life?"[6] Dom Vonier begs for psychological sincerity—no human has any idea what it would be like to live without a body, so a little more circumspection about how wonderful it would be to be "freed" of it is probably in order.

When we start to become aware of and embrace our bodies as really us, we can live into the bodily experience of life dynamically again, as we did spontaneously when we were young. We will all have our illnesses, our limitations, our aging, and yes, our bodily death.

---

[5] Dom Justin McCann, *The Resurrection of the Body* (Macmillan, 1928), 60-61.
[6] Anscar Vonier, *The Life of the World to Come* (Burns, Oates, and Washbourne, 1932), 164.

But we can experience all those things as exactly part of the way life goes, the way a whole human being lives on the earth, finding the wisdom present in the body's changing and aging over time. And we can also hope simultaneously for the age to come in which our bodies will no longer know these limitations, holding that eternal day close to the fragility of our bodily rhythms as we venture through our days and years.

Getting deeply back into our bodies also tends to help us see the ways we're connected with other creatures. The air we breathe, the food we eat, the water and other liquids we drink: our bodies are porous to the world. The world weaves in and out of us and we weave in and out of the world every moment of every day. We not only take, we give. We sometimes give back by growing a garden or caring for a pet, raising crops and tending livestock. But we also give back in our exhaled breath, in our waste (though we tend to avoid thinking about that), and one day our bodies will go back to the earth and become food for other creatures. That is, until the "blink of an eye, at the last trumpet" (1 Cor. 15:52) at any rate.

This might be well and good, but what does it all have to do with contemplation? We can be grounded in our bodies in life-affirming and healthy ways without having much to do with contemplation. And we should be. But the point here is that, if we contemplate, we contemplate as bodies+souls.

The tradition has long tended to the soul as the only really meaningful participant in contemplation, a bias built in from classical thought. If you go read the ancient and medieval treatises on prayer, contemplation, or mysticism you'll see all kinds of talk of the soul, of the different faculties and activities of the mind, but not much if anything on the body's role in the life of prayer and especially in contemplation. But it doesn't have to be this way.

St. Irenaeus—remember him?—said something that is another inspirational quote circulating online. In the usual form, it goes "The glory of God is a human fully alive." That's more or less what Irenaeus said, but a more literal translation of the Latin would be "The glory of God is a living human."[7] And as we know now, for Irenaeus it goes without saying that a "living human" is a body taken from the earth and a soul breathed into that body by the Spirit.

Still wondering what this has to do with contemplation? Well, the second half of that line doesn't get as much press but it's "and the life of a human is the vision of God." The foundation of our life is beholding God, and that life exists in a body+soul together. So when we consciously participate in that beholding, that vision—what the tradition has long called contemplation in a special use of that word—the whole person is doing something, is *living,* even if the soul is the part of us with a special, active role in that beholding.

Let's get more directly to it. I said above that when the body moves, it's the soul's activity that makes it move. William of Saint-Thierry, a twelfth-century Benedictine abbot who will come up a lot in these pages, said that the soul is in the body like God is in creation. That is, the soul is present in every part of the body, and wholly present in every part of the body. The soul is not limited by the body, but rather pervades it as it vivifies it. The body and soul are so integral to one another that St. Thomas Aquinas made clear that a human "soul" enjoys heaven or suffers hell after the body's death, not a "whole human."[8] The "whole human" (Latin: *totus homo*) will only experience heaven after the resurrection, when the body and soul are reunited. So even when the soul does what is special to it, the body is immediately and profoundly involved. William of Saint-Thierry also had something to say about this. As he summarizes the different activities of the soul in his book *The Nature of the Body and the Soul,* he notes that even when the soul is rapt in contemplation in such a way that it does not sense what is happening in the body, it

[7] Irenaeus of Lyons, *Against Heresies,* IV.20, 490.

[8] Thomas Aquinas, *Commentary on the Letters of Saint Paul to the Corinthians* (The Aquinas Institute for the Study of Sacred Doctrine, 2012), 15.2.924, 349. For clarity: "...the soul, since it is part of man's body, is not an entire man, and my soul is not I."

still, without recognizing it, is sensing everything and is still vivifying the whole body.[9] If it were not, the body would cease to live.

This is the crucial difference between the soul being "somewhere in" the body and controlling it like a crane operator on the one hand and the soul being wholly present everywhere in the body simultaneously on the other. The soul cannot *not* be intimately and integrally acting throughout the body as long as the body is alive. So even when we are engaged in contemplation, the body has an immediate role to play; it is present. We might say that the body is the witness of contemplation. This is especially good to keep in mind when the life of prayer moves into more exceptional states from time to time and bodily sense occasionally slips away for a while. (Perhaps the preoccupation with such exceptional states is what led many spiritual masters to pretty much ignore the body's role when discussing contemplation.) Despite what we are conscious of at any given moment: body+soul together.

But there is more. In addition to this immediate but mysterious presence to the soul's contemplative activity, the body has a significant role in preparing us for contemplation as well. The monastic tradition as passed down to us from the fifth-century monk St. John Cassian (who transmitted Desert monastic wisdom to the west) is abundantly clear here. For in St. John's *Conferences,* in which he reports the teachings of the Desert Fathers he visited, he begins with a teaching about the goals of the contemplative life. There, Abba Moses explains that what we are seeking in the life of prayer is "purity of heart" (for it is the pure of heart who will see God, Mt. 5:8). But generally, we can't just *do* that—though God's grace can take us by surprise in this regard sometimes too. Most of the time, to purify our hearts we have to practice. Grace is always assumed in this understanding of the life of prayer, but we have to accept and work with grace to sustain this life.

---

[9] William of Saint-Thierry, "The Nature of the Body and the Soul," in *Three Treatises on Man,* ed. Bernard McGinn (Cistercian Publications, 1977), 101-52 at 142.

And so Abba Moses makes the point that we fast, we keep vigil (staying up late praying), read the Scriptures, and do other disciplines in order to purify the heart. He adds that, if these practices do not support that purity of heart (and the contemplative beholding of God by implication), they are worthless. The point isn't to fast; the point is to become humble and to develop an undivided heart made for love of our Creator and of our neighbor. The early monks discovered that, as a general rule, fasting helped make that transformation possible. They discovered that staying up late to pray and depriving themselves of comfortable sleep helped too. They discovered that meditating on the Scriptures—and early on this "meditating" really meant repeating verses over and over—helped too. When these practices stopped helping, they were not to continue, for they were not ends in and of themselves.

Here in the practices of the bodily disciplines we find the body's integral and necessary role in the contemplative life for the early monastics. If you have not tried fasting or vigils or *lectio divina* as prayerful disciplines, I do recommend it, keeping in mind of course your own safety especially in the case of fasting. If we view fasting merely as "not eating sometimes" or as some sort of fitness regimen, the road to purity of heart is unlikely to open. But if we view it, if we live it, as a discipline that helps us see more clearly how dependent we are on other creatures to survive, how fragile our lives are, and if it helps us identify and empathize with those who have fewer of the earth's gifts than we do, it will become for us a royal road leading to purity of heart. If we see staying up late to pray as a drudgery, we will likely not find there a road to purity of heart. If we see it as a pledge of our fidelity and willingness to deny ourselves, take up our cross, and follow the Lord, it will also become for us a royal road leading to purity of heart. The same for *lectio divina* and the constant meditation of the Scriptures in our minds and hearts and on our tongues.

I would add to these traditional disciplines the turning of our awareness to our bodies in all their splendor. If we do this to delight our own vanity, we will not find a road to purity of heart. But, if we can find in our own bodies temples of the Holy Spirit, a holy sense of the living flesh animated by the soul and sustained by God's grace, destined to see that God face to face in eternity, we will find that royal road to purity of heart. Likewise, a turning of our awareness to other creatures and the earth itself. In our present selfish mode of walking the earth, of taking far more than we need and depriving other creatures made by the Creator the necessities of life, contemplation must turn toward them with compassion and a willingness to convert the heart. (I'll have more to say on this in a later chapter.) If we turn our gaze to the earth only to see what we can get from it, what we can control and dominate, we will not find a road to purity of heart. But if we can find there a real home again, if we can see every other creature on the earth as "a caress of God,"[10] we can find the royal road to purity of heart. These are embodied practices that also link us to others' bodies.

We shouldn't shrink away from these practices because they are difficult or in deference to "spiritual" works. After all, the western contemplative tradition is shaped foundationally by belief in the second Person of the Trinity becoming incarnate for our sake, and we too are called "to offer [our] bodies as a living sacrifice, holy and pleasing to God, [our] spiritual worship" (Rom. 12:1). Whether we will or no, the body cannot, will not be denied.

[10] Pope Francis, *Laudato Si'*, https://www.vatican.va/content/francesco/en/encyclicals/documents/papa-francesco_20150524_enciclica-laudato-si.html, §84.

SEEING THE WATER'S SURFACE CLEARLY: ON THE SOUL IN CONTEMPLATION

O God, you are my God—
it is you I seek!
For you my body yearns;
for you my soul thirsts…
Ps. 63:2

The Carolingian monk Smaragdus of Saint-Mihiel passed a poignant image from the early Desert monastic tradition on to later western monastics. At the end of a chapter on contemplation in his *Crown of Monks*, Smaragdus gives us this brief observation:

> A certain father said, "Just as it is impossible to see one's face in water that is stirred up, so also the soul can only pray contemplatively to God if it has been purged of alien thoughts."[1]

This sums up the basic movement (or lack of movement) of contemplation—in this case the contemplation in prayer oriented directly toward God.

When we look in a stream and the water moves over rocks and tumbles against curves in its banks, it is difficult

[1] Smaragdus of Saint-Mihiel, *The Crown of Monks*, trans. David Barry (Cistercian Publications, 2013), 62.

to see one's face clearly. But when the stream is languid and flowing smoothly, it is as if the surface is not moving at all. We can see ourselves when we look—though not exactly a mirror image, as colors reflected in water are often somewhat off and lighting plays tricks. Similarly, when the soul is stirred up by "alien thoughts"—the rocks of attachment and curving banks of unchecked attention given over to selfish desires, anxieties, and seemingly endless novelties—it too cannot see clearly to itself nor, ultimately, God. The point of so much contemplative practice is to still the body and discipline the soul's attentions so that the soul can "see" clearly as the body rests. Even when the body+soul achieves this clarity of vision and realizes the most "spiritual" contemplative states, what is seen is not the fullest picture; as bounded creatures we cannot know God as God knows God's self.

But what *is* the soul? When we talk like this, what on earth does it mean?

I was once teaching a summer class on female mystics and visionaries, and things were going okay. "Okay" because the students were doing the reading and trying to make sense of things, but it just wasn't hitting right. I don't recall now what was said, but suddenly during one strained conversation a stray comment set the proverbial light bulb off in my head. I stopped what we were doing, looked up at all of them, and asked squarely: "Do you guys know what the soul is?" They looked at one another, daring each other to give an answer, or maybe just pleading! But eventually, one brave young woman said, "We have no idea." So we took some time to walk through what the soul is in the long Christian tradition, and class started going a whole lot better. I started looking more and more into descriptions of the soul myself, and everything the ancient and medieval authors say about prayer and even about mortification started making even more sense to me as well.

So here's the run down, according to western spiritual writers from St. Irenaeus to the Benedictine Dame Gertrude More and beyond. You know when you think? That's the soul thinking. When you remember? That's the soul remembering. When you imagine a purple elephant with a star on its forehead? That's the soul imagining a purple elephant with a star on its forehead. Bottom line: anything that we think of as "mind" was the soul, until the modern era. Thinkers like René Descartes, Thomas Hobbes, John Locke, and David Hume gradually separated the soul from the body and left the soul aside as they described the world in more and more material terms, opting increasingly for "mind" as a preferred description of our psychic lives over "soul." As they did so, even people who continued to believe in the soul in the modern world lost a clear sense of what exactly it is, beyond "that part of us that keeps living after death" or "our essence" or general notions like these.

But there's more. The soul is also what senses the world around us. When you hear? That's the soul hearing. When you see this page and its type? That's your soul seeing this page and its type. When you taste? That's the soul tasting. When you feel a touch? That's the soul feeling a touch. The body has sense organs that take in sensations from the world around us, but it's the soul that actually perceives those sensations, since the body is inert matter without the soul. Animals share these aspects of the soul with us, as they are sensitive and can move themselves voluntarily. This way of thinking about the soul goes back at least to Aristotle, and has parallels in the Scriptures, enough that the Church Fathers kept right on teaching it. What is special about humans in this way of understanding ourselves is not that we have souls, but that we have souls that also have highly developed reason and the capacity for discernment and self-reflection in ways or to degrees that other animals don't. Embracing this teaching might just help us start to see other animals that walk the earth with us as kin, by the way. But that's for later.

There's even more. Even nourishment, growth, and reproduction are the work of the soul. Again, for this traditional way of looking at the world, the body is inert matter without the soul (that's why it decays at the separation of body+soul we call death). So when you grow, that's the soul getting the body to grow. When your organs work, that's the soul making the organs work. When you reproduce, that's your soul making the reproduction happen. (If there is any better argument for why we ought to respect our own and others' bodies, why sexuality is sacred and should be chastely lived, I don't know it.)

What this all gets us to is that the soul is all about *life*. The soul (*anima* in Latin) *animates* the body. Some authors even refer to the soul as "life" (*vita* in Latin). Really, the body isn't even a body unless the soul is present to animate the matter into tissues and organs, all working harmoniously in ways that empirical science cannot explain (as I mentioned above in the last chapter). By the way, we also share these powers with plants. Yes, that's right, Aristotle to St. Augustine to St. Hildegard of Bingen to St. Thomas Aquinas and his teacher St. Albert the Great and beyond all held that plants have souls. Souls with "vegetative" powers. Again, reclaiming this way of understanding souls might just help us see our plant neighbors as kin again too. More on that later as well.

So, the soul has lots of powers, lots of effects. The soul is what organizes the body and makes it grow, what moves the body and senses the world around us, and what reasons, imagines, remembers, wills, and intuits. (Intuition will come back strong in a moment.)

Take a moment quick to move your hand. Watch it. Try to recognize there the soul's movement. Not—as I noted in the last chapter and I think is worth repeating—that the soul sits up in the head or something and controls the body like a puppet master. Rather, as William of Saint-Thierry said, "The soul is in its body somewhat as God is in the world. Everywhere, and everywhere entire. It is entire in each sense, so that the entire soul senses in each; it is entire in each part, so that the entire soul gives vegetative and animal life to the whole body."[2] The soul is there animating the body, the soul is willing the movement. Take a moment and listen to whatever sounds are around you. The hearing ear brings in sensations of soundwaves, but

[2] William of Saint-Thierry, "The Nature of the Body and the Soul," 141.

it is the soul that is hearing what you're hearing right now. That's not the body, in this way of looking at who we are. But the soul *needs* the body to do that. As William also said, the soul thinks, but it needs the tongue to speak.

Unfortunately, the traditional take on all this tends to value the soul more than the body. But there is also latent in all this a sense that the body and the soul only really fulfill themselves when they are together: body+soul. If you and I can really become conscious of this dynamic union in our daily living, all of life becomes strangely, well, lively. Strangely present and *real*. We're not "sitting in our heads"—we're vibrantly living in all our tissues, all our sense impressions, all our thoughts and swirling mental images, the soul pervading the body, making a vital identity that is spiritual as well.

Paradoxically, when Descartes and Locke collapsed the soul into the mind, this diminished not just the body but the soul too. The body was made a puppet or a machine made of meat. And the soul, rather than being the pervasive animating force that unfolds the body's life, making all our biological processes happen in all their dizzying complexity and sensing the world—all *in addition to* the wonders of our minds' powers—the soul became the mind became just the thinking and calculating thing up in our head. The soul is so much more.

And yet, the soul on its own is also only a shadow of the person, as I noted in the last chapter. That's why our bodies, according to the most ancient tradition of the Church, are reconstituted and revivified at the Resurrection—we're a body+soul now and will be again at the end. The tradition holds that the body needs the soul, and the soul needs the body. Together they make a human person. This is also what our friend St. Irenaeus meant when he spoke of the "living human being" being the "glory of God": the Creator making the soul to live, the soul animating matter to form a living person. That is a miracle that is also just everyday reality.

So, what does this view of the soul have to do with contemplation and with our opening image of the stirred-up water? The answer, in short, is about stilling the water. We'll look at what the tradition has to say about different contemplative "states" in later chapters, from what we call "recollection" to what we call "unitive or mystical experience." Here the basic goal is to illuminate what the soul does in contemplation and how it relates to our common, everyday experience.

What contemplation *is not* is the soul forcing itself to "not think." I hear this complaint fairly regularly when I talk about contemplative prayer and meditation with people. They just can't stop themselves from thinking, and so they can't "get into" contemplative prayer, contemplation, or meditation. The problem is, the terms of that argument assume things about us as conscious creatures and about contemplation that are problematic. The point of contemplation is not to force yourself to stop thinking.

Part of the problem here gets back to the general problem I noted in the opening chapter and the modern shift from "soul" to "mind" to "thinking and calculating thing." The notion that discursive thought (when we're thinking with concepts and language) simply *is* our conscious, intelligent life is a relatively new one. And this notion is constantly reinforced for us by our constant attention to words (written and spoken) and images. And the way we talk about ourselves, about work, and about intelligence itself draws on this assumption and reinforcement, even when we don't realize it. The earlier western tradition, despite its faults, got one thing very right about us: our minds are not simply reasoning machines.

From Plato to Aquinas and later, "reason" was a distinguishing aspect of what it is to be a human. (And remember that in this way of looking at us, our minds, including reason, are just aspects of the soul.) But there was also the *understanding* (*intellectus* in Latin) which was a receptive, aware, but intuitive and simple way of apprehending and knowing. When we are awake and aware and yet not reasoning, the understanding is doing its thing. When we take in a moment or walk and simply *know* what we're doing, this is the understanding doing its thing. When we reason our way to new knowledge, that new knowledge lives in the understanding. And the understanding relies on contemplation to "see" the world simply. When we fill our physical and mental lives with words and images and sounds and more words and more images and more sounds, we constantly reinforce the reasoning, discursive mind and our ego's identification with that reasoning, discursive mind as well as our exteriorizing our sense of self through the senses. But that's not the whole story of who we are cognitively, let alone spiritually. We have the understanding (I avoid calling it the "intellect" because of how we think about the closely related term "intelligence" these days).

We see this gap in self-understanding rear its ugly head in our discomfort with and inability to explain the inaccuracy of the equation of human and machine "intelligence." When boosters talk about machine "intelligence" being equivalent (or superior) to human intelligence, they're using a very particular definition of intelligence that is about capacities to solve particular kinds of problems and that's all. But the human organism is more than a problem-solving machine made out of tissues. The conscious experience of a first-person perspective that grows, matures, and eventually dies is not a system of problem-solving. *To be aware is not to solve a problem.*

But it can be very difficult for us to see this in the world we live in, consumed as it is with efficiency, optimization, profit, and productivity. What is not quantifiable is not valued, and we can only see what we can see. If we lack a sense of the value of simple awareness—a kind of "festival awareness"—of an understanding that is not comprised of rational processes, it will be difficult to see how my mind can enter into contemplative awareness at all—this is the bitter fruit of quantification bias.

What's the practical point of all this? To cut to it: when I sit for fifteen minutes to devote myself to contemplative prayer, there are thoughts. Thoughts come, thoughts go. I can acknowledge those thoughts and say "I'm thinking, so now I can't be contemplating at all; it's a zero-sum game!" Americans especially like to think of everything as zero-sum games. But we can also simply be aware that the discursive mind is indeed having thoughts, and also not identify our whole mind with those thoughts. When we do so, we tend to begin having fewer thoughts. And the more time that goes by devoted to contemplative awareness, often the fewer thoughts that arise, leading to a gradual absorption of the mind into its own simplicity, without movement. This is stilling the water. This is when the soul can see other creatures outside itself in contemplation and starts to "see" itself in contemplation. Though contemplation can still be happening while the thoughts proceed, too, if we don't identify with them, hold onto them, and obsess over them. They'll arise. They'll pass. The mind is more than its thoughts. It's like St. Romuald says in his Brief Rule: "Watch your thoughts like a good fisherman watching for fish." Your thoughts aren't *you,* nor your mind, nor your soul. They are movements within the soul, the moving water that troubles one's view. But they'll settle out. And even if they don't, the water is still what it is even when there are ripples. Pay them no mind.

Dame Gertrude More has something to say about this in her description of her own spiritual life as she started practicing contemplative prayer. Though well intentioned, her spiritual director had been promoting formal meditations and intensive examinations of conscience, which nearly broke her and led to a crisis in her vocation to the monastic life. But when she began receiving instruction from Dom Augustine Baker, things changed:

> But God showed to me plainly in reading Father Baker's books that my way was to overcome myself as I could, not as I would, but expect God's good pleasure in it.... Which was a quite contrary course to that which was extolled by all that I ever met with before, who can give for the most part no other advice than to overcome all things by force and violence.[3]

She goes on to note how this way of practicing (doing what she *could*

[3] Dame Gertrude More, *Poems and Counsels on Prayer and Contemplation* (Gracewing, 2020), 39.

rather than what she *would*) also helped her maintain a clear view of her own ability in the spiritual life.

As we sit waiting in contemplative prayer, we often find ourselves thinking and wanting other things. To get fed up with this state of affairs is to subtly reject what grace God might provide. To embrace one's own weakness and inability to achieve great feats of contemplation (whatever we think that might mean) but do it anyway, offers us a way to practice the virtue of humility over and over again. As Saint Romuald says in his Brief Rule again: "Empty yourself completely and sit waiting, content with the grace of God, like the chick who tastes nothing and eats nothing but what his mother brings him."

The soul contemplates, whether that is a brief moment of simple awareness while sitting in a park at dusk or a life-shattering loss of bodily awareness and an intuition of the divine nature itself. But getting back to our commitment to seeing the body+soul as a whole—what happens to our body during contemplation, if contemplation is "done" in the soul? During those brief moments of simple awareness, the body usually calms down, relaxes as much as it can, and can provide surprisingly fulfilling spontaneity. The fact that the body does this during contemplation gives us a clue as to how to go about "practicing" contemplation—if we do with the body what usually happens to the body naturally during contemplation, we just might enter into contemplation more deliberately and more often. That's discipline. But we'll get to that in a later chapter.

If we want to probe more, we might ask what happens to the body when the soul is in a drastically altered contemplative state—if bodily awareness is gone, how can we say that the body has a role in contemplation at all? The whole tradition has a kind of quiet answer to this, but the only person I've seen address it head on, as intimated above, is William of Saint-Thierry. William notes in his book on the natures of the body and the soul that:

> Hence it is that even while it administers the body and gives it sensation, if at any time it raises itself through the internal gaze

> of the mind to high and eternal truths, it in a certain way leaves the bodily senses and ceases to be localized by them, so that it does not see things placed before them, does not hear sounds in the vicinity, does not understand the page the eyes are reading. By a marvelous and in a way God-like power, it is at the same time completely present in contemplating heavenly things by discernment, completely present in the sensation or act by which it is acting (although it does not sense what it does), and completely present in the body which it is vivifying. It is the same soul which senses: the same which does not understand what it senses: the same which, neither sensing nor understanding, quickens and vivifies the body through which it senses what through itself it does not understand.[4]

This way of understanding the human person holds that the soul is not simply "in the head" or "in the heart," nor that the soul or the mind direct the body like a puppet master, but rather is everywhere present in the body vivifying it. And so, even when contemplation reaches to extreme states, the soul is still wholly "present" in the whole body, otherwise the body would not live, would not continue its normal, everyday processes. But wouldn't you know it, when we have those life-shattering contemplative experiences, we "come back" to find that our bodies are doing just fine. Our bodies+souls are living together in all that we do until the body's death. There's an ominous ring to that, but also great comfort in the radical integrity of our life. In this way, again, I'd say that our bodies are faithful witnesses to our contemplation.

So: as the body grows quieter, and the discursive mind grows quieter, the contemplative mind, the understanding (*intellectus*) comes more into view. It's not that the understanding is not present when the discursive mind is doing its thing, or when the body is sensing the world around us. But the senses and the thinking mind

[4] William of Saint-Thierry, "The Nature of the Body and the Soul," 142.

can garner so much of our awareness that it becomes difficult to see that this other precious aspect of who we are is always there waiting to come back to the fore. In contemplation it's not that we go "out of ourselves," but rather we come back home and settle in most comfortably within all that we are.

ON THE UNITY OF BODY+SOUL

We're going to get to a provocative take on how contemplation is like orgasm pretty soon, so hang in there. First, a little context.

Way back in the fourth century BCE, Plato said that our bodies are a prison for our souls. Even though the Church inherited from ancient Judaism a more balanced and earthy valuation of our bodies, this Greek inheritance was difficult for even the Church Fathers to shake. As they affirmed that Christ had a real human body and that one day all the dead would be raised and live bodily forever, they devalued the body frequently and regularly talked about the body limiting or dragging down the soul, especially when they talked about contemplation "lifting up" the soul. (See the second-century *Sentences of Sextus* for example, or the eleventh-century *Meditations* of Guigo I the Carthusian, for condensed teachings that trend toward devaluing the body.) So there's been an undercurrent of our bodies not really being us all along, despite what the Church holds to be true about who we are.

Then at the dawn of what we call the modern world, René Descartes speculated that the mind (the soul) is some other substance not intrinsically related to the body but "using" the body like a machine. Once materialism and the mechanical understanding of biology became dominant among scientists and in larger society, even those who think there's nothing "spiritual" about us often talk as if the body is not really us. How we could not really be our bodies if nothing exists beyond the physical world is confounding to say the least. But we've now come to a place where people can debate, if there's any room for debate, whether we are a body *with a soul* or a soul *with a body*. It's difficult for folks to see that we could be both a body *and* a soul, not really us at all without both of these aspects of ourselves living together in unity.

Against all that, we can say that the body+soul is indeed a unity. This truth strikes a holy, life-affirming balance between a hyper-spiritualized view of ourselves on the one side and a materialist reduction of ourselves on the other. Cognitive science tells us that the mind is always an embodied mind. As practitioners constraining themselves to empirical methods, cognitive scientists can't assert a soul that could live beyond a body. But I am no scientist. Foundationally, biology can't explain definitively what it is to *be alive* rather than not, so I'll take that as my escape hatch to say without apology: the body+soul that we are is a unity. Mutually forming each other. At play with each other, if we can get a grasp on ourselves through discipline, through humility, through self-understanding. (Often at odds if we can't.) No matter how "disembodied" we feel so often, or how "weighed down" we feel so often, the human body+soul is a wonder, a sad, beautiful, blissful wonder.

Hugh of St. Victor wrote a stand-alone treatise on this unity in the twelfth century. It's rough going; you can tell he's straining to make some kind of orderly sense out of this mystery that we are. To his credit, he was very likely addressing some conflicts that were very much of his day. More or less (drawing on St. Augustine largely), he shows how aspects of our bodies are increasingly "spiritual" when we look at them properly. The imagination's impressions "touch" the soul's reason—the point of contact. The body flows into those impressions, as does the soul. But it's not really satisfactory in the end. St. Thomas argued instead for what philosophers call "hylomorphism"—basically, that the soul is the "form" of the body. This view says it's not that they're two different things really: the two can't really be divided from one another because they're one *thing*. The only division possible is the terribly traumatic rupture of bodily death.

Even then, the soul yearns to be reunited with the body until the resurrection. But that's really philosophical and difficult to understand unless you care to dive into what Aristotle had to say. Even then, it will always remain pretty abstract.

As you can probably guess by now, I prefer a twelfth-century monastic writer's take. The Carthusian monk Guigo II wrote a treatise called *Ladder of Monks.*[1] In the midst of his description of the effects of contemplation, our Guigo II has a surprising comparison to make:

> So the soul…inflames its own desires, makes known its state, and by such spells it seeks to call its spouse. But the Lord…does not wait until the longing soul has said all its say, but breaks in upon the middle of its prayer, runs to meet it in all haste, sprinkled with sweet heavenly dew, anointed with the most precious perfumes, and He restores the weary soul…. And just as in the performance of some bodily functions the soul is so conquered by carnal desire that it loses all use of the reason, and man becomes as it were wholly carnal, so on the contrary in this exalted contemplation all carnal motives are so conquered and drawn out of the soul that in no way is the flesh opposed to the spirit, and man becomes, as it were, wholly spiritual.[2]

In case you didn't pick up on this one, "some bodily functions" means "orgasm."

Though Guigo draws a pretty stark opposition between what is "earthly" and what is "spiritual" throughout his work, he betrays the poignant unity of the two when he compares the kind of unified experience of ourselves that we realize in orgasmic climax with the

[1] If you've ever heard about the steps of *lectio divina* as being comprised of *lectio* (reading), *meditatio* (meditation), *oratio* (prayer), and *contemplatio* (contemplation), this is the book that came from.

[2] Guigo II, *Ladder of Monks and Twelve Meditations,* trans. Edmund Colledge, OSA and James Walsh, SJ (Liturgical Press, 1981), 73-74.

kind of unified experience of ourselves we realize in contemplation (especially the "deeper" kinds). Guigo is caught up in an oppositional system that had its reasons for existing (going back to Plato and the like, as we've seen), but that made it difficult for him to see how the two kinds of unity might be more akin than he suspects. In the midst of climax, there is a suspension of the discursive thought that "spreads out" the mind and ignores the body. In contemplation there is a suspension of the discursive thought that "spreads out" the mind and ignores the body. I don't want to go so far as to say that sexual climax is contemplative in and of itself, but I for one also won't dismiss the possibility out of hand.

Both orgasm and (especially "mystical") contemplation have been understood to be "ecstatic" ("standing outside of oneself") experiences for millennia. Maybe instead of "standing outside of ourselves," we're really just experiencing the unity of all our faculties—somatic, sensual, mental, spiritual—in ways that are so foreign to our day-to-day experience as fallen human beings that it can seem like we must be "beyond" ourselves somehow. The realization of and abiding in our creaturely unity is for many an ego-shattering and sometimes life-altering experience.

This is the glorious nature of St. Irenaeus's "living human" whose unity of life is "the vision of God." This unity also sounds to me a lot like what St. John Cassian and the Desert Fathers and Mothers called "purity of heart"—another translation is "an undivided heart." Maybe to get back to the bedrock of the tradition, we could call ecstatic experience, unitive experience, an experience of an undivided and expansive heart.

THREE MOVEMENTS OF CONTEMPLATIVE PRAYER AND PRACTICES TO SUPPORT IT

Gregory the Great says that contemplation is a "loving knowledge."[1] How can this be? What does it mean? The Greek and Latin words for contemplation (*theoria* and *contemplatio*) both suggest vision. A vision having religious overtones, but a seeing regardless. Knowledge is like seeing when it beholds its object in a simple way. Contemplation does not *reason about* its object but *rests* in it, as Catholic philosopher Josef Pieper puts it, following Thomas Aquinas.[2] In this simple apprehension, it is like seeing, which rests in its object, not searching for it. And it is a loving knowledge in that it is a resting in what *is*, what is present, an affirmation of what exists, rather than abstraction from sense experience or a logical manipulation of information about something. It is the mind's embrace of what exists, of the Real, of the positivity of what is rather than what is not.

This loving knowledge can come in many different guises. While contemplation is often thought of—when it is thought of at all—as lofty, exceptional things that one supposes monastics do hidden away in their retreats, it is really a very common experience. When the discursive thought of the reason, the flights of the imagination, the recallings of the past all settle down and the understanding (the

---

[1] Gregory the Great, *Moral Reflections on the Book of Job*, X.VIII.13. Dom Jean Leclercq has a wonderful passage on this in his book *The Love of Learning and the Desire for God* (Fordham University Press, 1982), 32-33.

[2] Josef Pieper, *Happiness and Contemplation*, 74.

intellectus) simply beholds what is present, what is Real, contemplation, that loving knowledge, is happening.

That might be when we sip coffee looking out a window in the morning, hearing wren-song splashing over the backyard, or a moment of talking with a friend at twilight, or peering into the dark as we lay waiting to fall asleep. That might be when we hear a particularly moving song or are arrested by a painting in a museum. Dom Cuthbert Butler tells us in his *Western Mysticism* that "there is contemplation that is a simple thing. This it is that the old writers mean, when they take for granted that contemplation is the natural aim and the normal issue of a spiritual life."[3] Pieper, too, says that "we need to know that the high appreciation accorded for so long to contemplation has every right to be accorded to a good many experiences which come our way in the course of everyday life. And we also need to know that we have a right to take the blessings of such experiences for what they truly are: foretaste and beginning of the perfect joy" of eternity.[4] Amen.

CONTEMPLATIVE PRAYER

Beyond the fleeting, everyday moments of contemplation, there is the practice of calling the powers of the mind together, and the ways in which contemplation moves into more and more "spiritual" or "internal" states, experiences that are exceptional and verge into what we often call mysticism. Every one of these places in the spectrum of contemplation are part of what it is to be human, since we are creatures of a Creator who made us to behold creation, ourselves, and even, yes, that Creator itself in our limited capacity.

Such contemplative experience also has the possibility of becoming *contemplative prayer* when we are aware of our relation with God, when we direct our contemplative rest and beholding toward our Creator, whatever the particular moment presents to us.

[3] Dom Cuthbert Butler, *Western Mysticism*, 271.
[4] Pieper, *Happiness and Contemplation*, 83.

As Dom Butler says, "By contemplative prayer is meant the kind of prayer in which or by which contemplation is exercised."[5] This may seem too obvious to state, but I think the strangeness or exceptional nature that is often attached to the words "contemplative prayer" today warrants saying it. Butler points out that to be called contemplative prayer, such moments should really be extended, but this is more a matter of attentiveness and willingness to give our time to such moments than about the exertion or strangeness of the experience of contemplation.

NO TECHNIQUE, BUT PRACTICE

If contemplative prayer is prayer in which contemplation plays a primary role (even as an intended goal), how do we start *doing* that? The first thing to say is that, like all discussions of Christian contemplative prayer, this one assumes a basic taking on of the yoke of discipleship. I'm not going to go into ways of loving one's neighbor in the very real contexts of everyday life, not because they are unimportant (of course they are), but because here we're trying to focus on one particular aspect of the spiritual life. I assume that if you're reading this and seeking to deepen your prayer life through contemplation, you're also striving to love your neighbor and love God, that you're trying to live that life how your tradition teaches, etc.

The second thing to say is that when Christian authors speak about contemplation they usually mean a contemplation that's intentionally oriented toward a person's inner life and toward God dwelling in the believer's heart. As I hope I've been making clear, there are also natural contemplation and aesthetic contemplation, and those are important too, given the modes of living our society tends to promote. But those have their own chapters, since they're less talked about by western spiritual masters. Here we're looking directly at how we can support the grace of contemplative prayer—contemplation

[5] Butler, *Western Mysticism*, 265.

directed in a prayerful way toward "beholding" the soul itself and the soul's Maker. This does not mean that other forms of prayer are inferior or unnecessary. Rather, this is one form of prayer, but one that gets at the deep-down aspects of the spiritual life and is regularly neglected in the modern world.

Since contemplation is part of how we're made, sometimes it happens spontaneously. But because this spontaneous activity is something we're made for (as we'll discuss more later), we can also cultivate that ground and enter into it more deliberately, more regularly. We can quiet the body, we can still the mind. This is what Gregory the Great calls "gathering ourselves." But is it prayer? I would argue that it's made to be prayer, it was intended by our Creator to be prayer, as all of life was intended to be prayer, our active union with the divine nature. But in the fallen world it doesn't necessarily work that way.

We can quiet the body, we can still the mind. We can enter into contemplation, with training and perseverance, pretty readily. But contemplation becomes prayer when that activity is opened out, in the will, toward God. Just like we can talk all day and never pray, when we move those words, in the will, toward God we begin vocal prayer. Contemplation is a great good in our lives, but it's not necessarily prayer until we orient it toward our maker. That doesn't mean we "think about God." It's a matter of the heart's direction and seeking. We might be entering into contemplation while watching our children play, while walking through a forest, while sitting silently in our inner room—but when our hearts are oriented toward our Creator we are at prayer.

When one longs to contemplate, to be simply in relationship with our Creator not as an idea or a concept but as the living God, we turn to contemplative prayer. But what is this turn? What does it look like? What do we do?

The first instruction regarding contemplative prayer is usually "there is no method for contemplative prayer." That's not very helpful on the surface, but we'll come back to it. Because there are things that we can do to dispose ourselves to contemplative prayer, to prepare our body+soul, our minds and hearts, for the simple beholding of the divine, when the "day dawns and the morning star rises in [our] hearts" (2 Pet. 1:19). St. Gregory tells us in his *Homilies on the Book of the Prophet Ezekiel* that when we set out in contemplative prayer, we ought to 1) gather ourselves, 2) then be attentive to the nature of that gathering in the soul, and 3) "by intention submit to the contemplation of the invisible Creator."[6] The general movement here is to quiet and center the body+soul, to be aware of that quiet and centered state of the body+soul (especially aware of the soul itself), and to reach out with the soul only to the source of all that is.

QUIET WITHIN AND WITHOUT

One step at a time. How do we "gather ourselves"? This is about "stilling the water" as we saw in an earlier chapter. How do we still the water? Plenty of ways, including the more general disciplines of fasting, vigils, and *lectio divina*. But, when we want to enter into contemplative prayer *right now*, there are a few tried and true practices. First, having quiet and solitude outside the body+soul. Not that silence and being alone are necessarily goods in and of themselves or that they are necessary for contemplation, but if we are to invite the discursive mind to settle down so the contemplative mind can come to the fore, the less sense stimulation the better. This is stilling the water. Having a place to sit in one's "inner room" is a big help here. It might be outside, it might be in a quiet room of the house or apartment, wherever, so long as one can have some access to quiet and stillness. (A note: if someone needs your help, please help them;[7] don't neglect them because this is "your" time for contemplative prayer. We can seek quiet and solitude without blocking others out.)

[6] Gregory the Great, *Homilies on the Book of the Prophet Ezekiel* (Center for Traditionalist Orthodox Studies, 2008), II.5.9, 339.
[7] Benedict of Nursia, *The Rule of St. Benedict*, 4:26.

POSITION

Part of this external quiet and solitude is also the body's own position and movement. Though the Christian world certainly doesn't have the intricate physical practices that developed in monastic circles in Hinduism and Buddhism, there are still guideposts. St. Benedict's invitation for those who desire to pray to linger in the oratory after the community has finished the Divine Office is one hint: given what we know about medieval prayer practices, a monastic presumably sat, knelt, or prostrated themselves in the quiet space of the oratory with few to no others around.[8] But we also have descriptions of monastics *sitting* alone in their cells all over the tradition. A little more specific direction comes from Richard Rolle, an English hermit of the fourteenth century:

> [I]f I wished to contemplate by standing or walking, or lying down, I saw that much was deficient and I was, it seemed, desolate...The act of sitting allows for wakefulness with the minimum of distraction. Thus, compelled by this necessity, I chose to sit down that I might have and persevere in the highest devotion. I did not ignore the cause of this, for if a person stands or walks for long, their body gets tired and thus the soul is hindered and to a certain degree challenged by that burden. And it will then be prevented from entering into its greatest silence and, as a consequence, lack perfection, for according to the Philosopher [Aristotle], "it is in sitting and remaining silent that the soul becomes prudent." Therefore, one who still delights more in standing than in sitting amidst divine realities should know that he is still far distant from the heights of contemplation.[9]

Richard doesn't tell anyone *you have to do it this way*, but explains why he finds it most conducive to contemplative prayer to sit:

[8] Benedict of Nursia, *The Rule of St. Benedict*, 52:2-5.

[9] Richard Rolle, *The Incendium Amoris of Richard Rolle of Hampole*, ed. Margaret Deanesly (University of Manchester, 1915), ch. 14, 185.

standing takes too much effort, laying down makes him tired. That's it. Similarly, the sixteenth-century Benedictine abbot Louis of Blois says "Some people can better engage themselves with God and more easily remain in contemplation sitting than standing or kneeling," perhaps suggesting that he is one of these people?[10] Dame Gertrude More, too, says that as she regularly resorts to "that unchangeable light" of the godhead, "it exceedingly rejoiceth me to sit down and sigh after thee."[11]

Do you have to stay totally still? No, there aren't any rules. Remember from above, there is no "method" for contemplative prayer. In my own initiation into monastic contemplative prayer, we had a whole hour of seated prayer twice a day. That's a lot for most bodies to take, so we would take a silent break half-way through to slowly walk in a ring for about five minutes before sitting again to conclude the hour. The break helped everyone maintain the physical ability to continue and gave the contemplative prayer a visceral social dimension too. Whatever supports the ability to sustain an openness to the Spirit in a contemplative mode.

MEDITATION/MENTAL REPETITION

The other aspect of Gregory's gathering is an internal quieting. As mentioned in the last chapter, forcing yourself not to think is not the plan and wouldn't work well for most of us even if it were. So what's to be done? The basic strategy in the Christian tradition goes all the way back to the desert. In desert monasticism, the mothers and fathers placed a central emphasis on the meditation of Scripture. And in that period, "meditation" meant primarily "repetition." So they would memorize the Scriptures and repeat them throughout the day. This gave them something to occupy the mind with that was spiritually nourishing in addition to being a practical help to "stopping thoughts."

St. John Cassian tells us about this practice in the mouth of

[10] Louis of Blois, *A Book of Spiritual Instruction* (Newman Press, 1955), 94.
[11] Dame Gertrude More, *Confessions of a Lover,* Confession 10.

Abba Isaac in his *Conferences*. Abba Isaac tells us to choose a verse of Scripture and repeat it over and over again. He says that the verse "O God, come to my assistance. Lord, make haste to help me" from Psalm 70 is the most perfect verse that his elders had passed on to his generation of monks. It was chosen from all of Scripture because "it takes up all the emotions that can be applied to human nature and with great correctness and accuracy it adjusts itself to every condition and every attack," and whoever calls out to the Creator constantly "is sure that he is always present."[12] This is the basic practice that the modern Benedictine John Main recommended in his revitalization of Christian meditation.

Abba Isaac further insists that this is a serious aid to contemplative prayer because not only does it focus the discursive mind on the Word of God but also because with the constant repetition the discursive mind doesn't get the chance to start off on its own wide-ranging thoughts. He insists on saying it whenever not occupied with some other mental task that must be done. He says to repeat it during work, and when tending to the duties of nature, to fall asleep to it and wake up to it. Basically, in doing so we give the thinking mind something to do that is repetitive but also spiritually nourishing so that the soul is being fed while getting the thinking mind out of the way. We also start to experience the Scriptures rather than only understanding them intellectually. Cassian's whole book is well worth a read. Anyway: if our minds want to say things, fine, let them say a verse of Scripture. And let them say it over and over so our intuitive, contemplative minds don't have to get dragged along for random rides. And let them say the Scriptures so as to be led in their path.

Later Benedictine authors, like Louis of Blois and Augustine Baker, apply a similar principle but will offer many other short prayers to say. Another more modern one that has deep roots in western monastic spiritual culture is the "ejaculatory prayer"

---

[12] John Cassian, *Conferences* (Paulist Press, 1997), 10.X.1-3, 379.

"Sacred Heart of Jesus, have mercy on us!" To pray for the Sacred Heart's mercy on us all as we wake, as we go about our business, as we fall asleep, as we straiten (and expand) the mind with a single intent, leads us to those beatitudes, "Blessed are the poor in spirit, for theirs is the kingdom of heaven" and "Blessed are the pure in heart, for they shall see God."

One primary western variation of this practice is found in the fourteenth-century English text, *The Cloud of Unknowing*. There, the anonymous author offers the practice of choosing a single word, the shorter the better, and repeating that word in our minds whenever we find ourselves starting to will anything but the simple, naked stretching of the will to God. No matter how many times we find ourselves thinking of what we have to do later this evening, or what some celebrity was wearing yesterday, what the politicians are up to, or how we'd rather be out playing tennis instead of sitting here doing nothing, we simply say the word and continue our simple attending to God's presence at the heart of all that is. Then when we start thinking about how good we are at that, we say it again. And again. It's a good lesson in humility. This is the version of the teaching that the Centering Prayer movement adopted.

WITH THE BREATH

One last practice for "gathering" ourselves before moving on. This one gets past the boundaries of the western Church, but it's too important not to mention. Fourteenth-century spiritual master St. Gregory Palamas famously defended the practices of Eastern Christian monks. In defending the "hesychastic" movement, he notes that those who are setting out on the contemplative path need specific practices to "gather" the soul, "to concentrate and reintegrate the distracted mind."[13]

Especially for beginners, the "Jesus Prayer" (an eastern development of the desert practice of repetitious recitation) is a primary help,

---

[13] Gregory Palamas, *The Triads* (Paulist Press, 1983), 125 n. 25. Gregory's treatment of the breath is found in C.7.

but so too is the training of the breath. He points out that the regular control of the breath serves to regulate the mind—noting too, as I did above, that this seems to help because when we enter into contemplative states the breath becomes smooth and deep. Reversing the process seems to help, because we are body+soul. The teachers he draws on recommend the reciting of the Jesus Prayer in time with the rhythm of the breath. This helps to concentrate and reintegrate the mind, allowing the contemplative mind to shine through in consciousness. He makes clear that this is primarily for beginners though, while those used to this way of prayer enter into contemplative states more spontaneously, as their body+soul is re-trained for this so as to make contemplative receptivity a habit. Again, there's no method to "make" contemplation happen. But some of these practices can help.

While I've not come across a premodern western master who recommends using the breath in this particular way,[14] breath (*spiritus* in Latin, which also means "spirit") crops up in some interesting places that are suggestive of the importance of breath in the spiritual life. William of Saint-Thierry, for one, discusses the most intimate exchanges between God and the soul in terms of lovers exchanging breath ("spiritus") in their kisses—the whole text is well worth a read.[15] And Dame Gertrude More composed a prayer in Latin in one of her works, a beautiful prayer that I've attached as an appendix to the end of this book, which ends "O true and only Sun! We adore you as you rise, we enjoy you as you shine, for we who are

[14] As this book goes to press, I've literally just stumbled upon St. Ignatius of Loyola's "Third Method of Prayer" ("By Rhythm") in the *Spiritual Exercises.* There, he explains how one can pray the Our Father or other similar prayers, mentally saying one word of the prayer with each breath. He says too that rather than giving primary attention to the word of the prayer, one might "let attention be given...to the person to whom [one] recites it, or to [one's] own baseness, or to the difference from such great height to [one's] own so great lowness" (David L. Fleming, *Draw Me into Your Friendship: The Spiritual Exercises, a Literal Translation and a Contemporary Reading* [St. Louis: The Institute of Jesuit Sources, 1996], 196). A fruitful but late addition.

[15] William of Saint-Thierry, *Exposition on the Song of Songs,* section 95.

insufficient ceaselessly fail. In you and through you may we breathe life, take breath in, and expel it."[16]

RHYTHM AND EXTENT

Finally, there is the temporal dimension. How long and how often? Most practitioners of contemplative prayer recommend two deliberate periods of time set aside for contemplative prayer a day, morning-and-eveningish. Most recommend at very least setting aside ten minutes, if not a solid twenty. Anything more is great. Like I said, at the monastery where I learned about contemplative prayer, Osage Monastery-Forest of Peace, Sr. Pascaline Coff had us set aside an hour for silent, contemplative prayer. There was one session each in the morning and evening, with an additional twenty minutes before lunch.

The idea here isn't that if you devote twenty minutes twice a day, you'll start having profound contemplative experiences. Again, there's no method to make contemplative prayer happen. Rather, we are always engaged in *askesis*—we are always training our body+soul for something, whether we mean to or not. So the two times a day practice is about providing some counter-training to what our society demands of us. It is about forming a habitual openness *to* contemplative prayer. If we're training our body+soul from the time we get up in the morning (or even before we get up, for plenty of folks) to the time we go to bed at night (or even after we go to bed, for plenty of folks) to give our attention to ideas, words, images on screens, text, concepts, always more ideas, words, images on screens, text, concepts, then we are fixing our body+soul on sensory stimulation and discursive mental states. The contemplative activity of the *intellectus* has difficulty getting any traction in that way of living. If we "gather" ourselves deliberately, a couple times a day, especially at hinge points of the day like dawn and the coming of evening, through silence, through removing machines from our vicinity, through simply being

[16] Dame Gertrude More, *Poems and Counsels*, 73.

present and aware, we will start to train the body+soul for something else—for inner peace, for quiet, for contemplation. And when this contemplation is directed toward God, it is a prayer of openness to the Spirit's movements.

DEVELOPING EARS TO HEAR

It is in this openness of heart to the Spirit that the transformation of the body+soul occurs. It's not that grace doesn't come our way anyway, but will we have ears to hear it when it calls? A life consumed with electronic messages, keeping up on all the ideas and words and videos that pile up day after day, with the making of money, makes it difficult to hear anything else. This is not a black-and-white choice; we can take part in society, including digital society, and still be a contemplative. But we have to put forth effort (discipline, *askesis*) if we are going to open up the contemplative dimension in our life as a balance to all the activity. That's how there can be practices to take on every day, and yet there is also no method of contemplative prayer.

One instructive example of this comes to us again from Dame Gertrude More. When she was being initiated into contemplative prayer, Dom Augustine Baker instructed her to leave off all the discursive meditations and the excessive examinations of conscience, and rather simply attend to God with her will. Interestingly, she says that the deliberate setting aside of time for contemplative prayer

> was only for an entrance, not for a continuance, since a soul well settled in prayer would not need it, though at first for four or five years a soul by being hindered from two serious recollections in a day by her superiors would have perhaps been in great danger of inconveniency of her progress.[17]

Just like St. Gregory Palamas, she contends that the more deliberate

[17] Gertrude More, *Poems and Counsels*, 32.

practices are needed at the beginning, and later one typically does not need them so much. Why? Because our body+soul is trainable. Once we have habitually opened up space in our lives for the contemplative dimension, we are aware of it and can attend to it much more readily. Just like we can readily pick up a smartphone and enter into the very particular mental state of the smartphone world once we've done it for a while. We train for what we want, or we don't and see what happens.

By the way, the earliest I can trace the explicit instruction of two times a day, morning and evening, for sitting in contemplative prayer is to Dame Gertrude's spiritual father Dom Augustine Baker, who notes in his instructions to the nuns under his spiritual direction that they should have two set "recollections" or sessions of "mental prayer," one at seven in the morning, the other at four in the afternoon. He also suggests that anyone who needs it can take time for a set period of "mental prayer" after Compline (the night office before retiring) as well.[18]

FLOWERING OF THE *INTELLECTUS*

Stilling the water of the soul primarily means letting the soul be free of images and concepts so that it can simply experience itself as it is in itself—seeing our face in the water. But what of the second movement of contemplative prayer, what Gregory calls "being aware of that gathering" of the self? As letting the discursive, rational mind settle down and experiencing the simple awareness of the *intellectus* begin to become more habitual and clear, we pass over from "natural" contemplation to what the long tradition has generally simply called "contemplation," but is really a special kind of contemplation that is particularly religious in nature.

This primarily means that grace is needed to continue down this path, at least for its further reaches. Teachers differ on where

[18] Augustine Baker, *Directions for Contemplation: Book D* (Institut für Anglistik und Amerikanistik, 1999), 47-48.

natural shades into supernatural contemplation. But I'm not concerned with strict systems and fine gradations. The pre-Victorine way (before Hugh and Richard started defining finely graded "steps" of the contemplative path in the twelfth century) saw that sometimes we engage in contemplation in relation to the natural world of creation, of which we are a part, and sometimes it became more "internal," more concerned with the soul itself and the "heavenly realities" that pass between the soul and God. This is when we start talking about turf that for the past few centuries has been called mystical contemplation.

This more obscure aspect of contemplation mostly takes place beyond the senses and beyond the rational mind's capacity to analyze directly. It's very much in the *intellectus*'s wheelhouse, when the other powers of the soul (sense, emotions, imagination, memory, reason, and will) have been gathered up and one's awareness becomes awareness of the soul itself. Gregory tells us of this aspect of contemplation that we become aware of the soul as it is in itself (the clear surface of the water where we see our reflection, not the ripples).

But why and how could such an awareness lead "to the contemplation of the invisible Creator"? Gregory expands on the movement he traces like this: "But one by no means composes himself unless he has first learned to curb the apparitions of earthly and heavenly images from his mind's eye and cast out and tread down whatever of sight, hearing, smell, touch, and taste occurs to his bodily thought, in order that he may inwardly seek what is free thereof."[19] Releasing images and thoughts enables the soul to see itself as it is, a simple spirit rather than a bundle of disparate and conflicting parts. "When therefore the soul thinks of herself without any bodily images she has already entered the first door [of contemplation]. But this door leads on to the other in order that something of the nature of almighty God may be contemplated." "The one makes all but is not divided in all. For he is truly the Highest and never unlike himself. But the

[19] Gregory, *Homilies on Ezekiel*, II.5.9, 339-40.

soul, although she is never diverse by nature, yet is diverse through thought." Here we see to the inner logic of the practice of contemplative prayer that focuses on quieting the inner movements of the mind. In this view, the soul's nature is simple (not a bunch of parts), but it becomes "diverse" (*experienced* as a bunch of parts) when all the soul's faculties are occupied doing things—making images, remembering events, forming and relating concepts, etc. If we get the water to settle, we experience the soul as it is by its nature. And, as a spirit, the soul is like God in being simple, not composed of parts. So the soul experiencing itself as simple and eternal becomes a window onto God, especially given that God dwells in the soul.

Dame Gertrude More might make this clearer, at least by repetition: "It sufficeth not for the soul that there is in God himself, whom the soul seeketh after, simplicity or unity. But there must also be all possible simplicity in the soul herself, for the making her fit to treat with God."[20]

The soul "seeing" itself as it is when not actively doing other activities opens out into the direct encounter with God in our similarity to the godhead in our spiritual nature. For the long tradition, this is as close as we get to experiencing the direct vision of the divine substance (the "beatific" vision) in this life. Though we can also see this closeness with new acuity in the more contemporary emphasis on the relational nature of all things in an ecological key (see Pope Francis's repeated reminder in *Laudato Si'* that "everything is connected"). I say more about that elsewhere though.

EMPTY YOURSELF AND SIT WAITING

So, in the act of contemplation: sometimes the kind of simplicity that Gertrude and Gregory describe happens in our conscious experience. Sometimes it's just peaceful and quiet in our body+soul. Sometimes it's just a nice break or rest. Sometimes it's really boring.

[20] Dame Gertrude More, *Poems and Counsels*, 45.

And from a Christian perspective founded in God's grace being all-important for not only our very life but for all our relationships, the variability and inability to know what to expect are simply the way it is. There is no *method* for making contemplative awareness of God happen.

We are used to machines and think of the world, other creatures, even ourselves functioning mechanically: do one action, watch the pre-ordained mechanical effect occur. The more we invite and encourage contemplative awareness in our lives, the more we realize how impoverished the mechanical view of the world and of ourselves is. Rather, there is life, there is grace, there is mystery, there is spontaneity, there is inscrutability that begets wonder and joy. But the practices of stillness (whether sitting or moving in slow, deliberate ways), silence (whether literal quiet or the disciplined use of the voice that is the liturgy or similar vocal prayer), and regular periods of practice daily, habituate us to notice our own contemplative dimension and open us to notice the grace that is offered to us. As St. Romuald says, "Empty yourself completely and sit waiting, content with the grace of God, like the chick who tastes nothing but what his mother brings him." For this to form an integral part of our lives, we generally have to *do* the sitting and waiting, again and again.

Thinking about it isn't doing it.

LIVING *SECUM*: ON RECOLLECTION

Where can I go from your spirit? From your presence, where can I flee?
Ps. 139:7

Somewhere between the seemingly random moments of heightened awareness and the exceptional glimpses of divine light beyond body awareness, there's the regular practice of gathering in the mind to the present moment. Every moment. Drawing the mind away from the past and future, the fantasies and wishes, the projection of the mind onto and into machines and devices. Drawing the mind to presence in the body, in the immediate surroundings, in the given moment, to our living as it is lived. This is, more or less, what the tradition calls "recollection."

To recollect is "to gather in again." Gabriel Marcel called this an "ingathering," and he saw it as the only real retreat from the habits of body+soul that our technique-driven, efficiency- and productivity-obsessed society trains us in. As we noted, St. Gregory the Great says so as well: the first step of contemplation is "to gather the self." As such, recollection is an aspect or a place in the spectrum of contemplation. It is the contemplative awareness that can be extended and practiced most deliberately and regularly. When we think about living a "contemplative life," we're generally thinking about having a habitual recollected awareness that informs (I mean that pretty literally) our actions, our choices, our responses to what the present moment offers us. In St. Benedict's description of the spiritual life in his Rule, recollection is described in terms of the *memoria dei,* "the memory or mindfulness of God." In his description of the twelve steps of humility, the first is that "while he guards himself at every moment from sins and vices of thought or tongue, of hand or foot, of self-will or bodily desire, let him recall that he is always seen by God in heaven, that his actions everywhere are in God's sight and are reported by the angels at every hour."[1]

We can see a fuller description of what this might look like in Gregory the Great's *Life of St. Benedict.* After Benedict lived as a hermit at Subiaco for several years, he was advancing in the spiritual life but still suffered from serious temptations. Once he was tempted by lust to such a painful degree that he stripped himself naked, threw himself into a briar patch, and rolled around until he was pierced and itching from head to toe. (Not recommended, but let's go with it as a dramatization of Benedict's preparedness to take on authority over others in the spiritual life.) After Benedict has his tumble in the thorns and thistles, he is invited to become a monastery's abbot. But the life of the community and Benedict's earnestness do not blend well, and his new monks try to poison him. After departing the monastery, he returns to his retreat at Subiaco "where he lived alone with himself but under the gaze of the Heavenly Spectator."[2]

What does this strange expression "with himself" (in Latin: *secum*) mean? Gregory explains that "every time we are drawn outside ourselves by too much mental agitation, we are not 'with ourselves,' even though we think we are. Because when we wander here and there we do not see ourselves."

[1] Benedict of Nursia, *The Rule of St. Benedict,* 7:12-13.
[2] Gregory the Great, *Life of St. Benedict,* 22.

Gregory explains that we can be outside ourselves by dissipation (below ourselves) or by deep contemplation (above ourselves). The spatial metaphor is of course just that: a metaphor. But the idea is that by our mental exertion, the powers of the mind—recall that in the tradition here "the mind" is the collective cognitive powers of the soul—are scattered. When they are scattered, the imagination, the senses, the reason, the memory, the will, are all off on their own adventures, and the self is—to use our own contemporary metaphor—all over the place. Living *secum*, "with oneself," is the spiritual act of drawing the powers of the mind together, pulling imagination, the senses, the reason, the memory, the will, all in unity with the *intellectus*, the understanding, to draw one's inner life into the present moment in the body, to face and encounter reality as a unity. Recollection is the sustaining of this activity through time.

How do we do this? How do we live with ourselves? Gregory tells us that Benedict "'lived with himself' because he was always on guard and watchful. He was always aware of being before the eyes of the Creator": "Venerable Benedict dwelt with himself in that solitude when he guarded himself in a mental cloister." While, if God is omnipresent, we cannot actually "not be present" to God, we can certainly lose awareness of ourselves as present to the divine and of God dwelling in us. Compare this description with Benedict's *memoria dei* above. To live with oneself is to have the faculties gathered together in the present moment, conscious of God's presence to us and our presence to God, the Heavenly Spectator.

Cistercian monk and author Thomas Merton puts this in more modern terms for us:

> We must be present to ourselves. The cares and preoccupations of life draw us away from ourselves. As long as we give ourselves to these things, our minds are not at home. They are drawn out of their own reality into the illusion to which they tend. They let go of the actuality which they have and which they are, in order to follow a flock of possibilities. But possibilities have wings, and our

> minds must take flight from themselves in order to follow them into the sky. If we live with possibilities we are exiles from the present which is given us by God to be our own, homeless and displaced in a future or a past which are not ours because they are always beyond our reach. The present is our right place, and we can lay hands on whatever it offers us. Recollection is the only thing that can give us power to do so.[3]

In learning to recollect ourselves regularly, we begin to experience ourselves, our surroundings, other people and other creatures, and even time with new eyes (physical and spiritual). For recollection is not something that we do in a room alone in silence. As we noted in the chapter on practice, having a couple sessions like that a day helps the grounding necessary for this continued recollection in activity, but the goal of that grounding and the constant meditation of Scripture or some short prayer is to extend that "ingatheredness" of moments devoted earnestly to silence and the inhabitation of the "inner chamber" of the heart to every moment of life. To "pray without ceasing" (1 Thes. 5:17). Sixteenth-century Benedictine abbot Louis of Blois tells us, one "who never seeks his own satisfaction or convenience, but looks at God through all things, adverse as well as prosperous, in order to tend purely and simply towards God, is able to perform all his outward actions without dissipation, and though occupied with many things, does not lose the unity of his mind, which seeks God alone in all things."[4] In imitation of the Incarnation itself, the spiritual life is not about becoming a pure spirit but about harmonizing body+soul so that our inner reality and our outer reality are unified and present throughout our days.

In this way, recollection contributes to the realization of the "living human" that St. Irenaeus says is the "glory of God." When we practice recollection regularly, the *memoria dei* (remembrance or mindfulness of God) infuses our bearing, our attitude, our way of

---

[3] Thomas Merton, *No Man Is an Island* (Dell, 1960), 212-13.
[4] Louis of Blois, *A Book of Spiritual Instruction*, 28.

seeing the world, our very physical movements. Body+soul move together ever more closely, contemplatively encountering each present moment, realizing each present moment as a sacrament or sign of eternity in communion with God, dwelling in our hearts.

THROUGH SLANTED WINDOWS: ON SENSITIVE GROUND

And with our eyes open to the deifying light and our ears astonished, let us listen to the divine voice daily calling out to us...
Rule of St. Benedict Prol.9 (my translation)

Much of human contemplation is pretty ordinary, very much about *a way of subjectively and cognitively encountering* our own experience and the world around us. But the Christian tradition takes up this contemplative way of being in the world and says that there is indeed more. Not only do we/can we see other creatures contemplatively, or our own inner world contemplatively, but through the gift of God's grace we can be "lifted up" (a spatial metaphor that I'm not terribly fond of because it seems to imply greater value via superiority) to spiritually *see* God even in this earthly life.

When early writers start talking about this, warnings tend to come up. Namely: this shouldn't be talked about with folks new to the spiritual path. While I'm not one for secrecy, as it tends toward elitism and power plays—I'm a democrat—I do see why such warnings are prudent. Primarily, one inexperienced in the rhythms and habits of the spiritual life developed through discipline and mortification may accept such graces as favors that confirm who they already are rather than as enticement to what they could be. On this score, William of Saint-Thierry tells us why our Creator permits to those "chosen and loved by God" such fleeting moments of access to the divine Light: "This is in order that what [one] is allowed to glimpse for a passing moment may set the soul on fire with longing for full possession of eternal light, the inheritance of full vision of God."[1]

St. Gregory the Great likewise points to the paradoxically unexceptional nature of such exceptional experiences in his commentary on Ezekiel 40:16, interpreting the "slanting windows" "round about" the guard chambers of the Temple:

> But whoever already concentrates on the light of contemplation must take great care always to guard his mind in humility and never exalt himself concerning the grace with which he is imbued, and consider the nature of the *slanting windows* which denote the minds of contemplatives. For light enters by slanting windows, and a thief does not enter, because those who are truly searchers always restrain their perception in humility, and the understanding of contemplation enters their minds but the bragging of elation does not."[2]

The light comes in "slanted," not directly, so no one has cause to boast. In addition, the windows are

> on every side round about [because] the grace of contemplation is not given to the greatest nor to the least, but often the greatest, often the least, receive it, but more often hermits and sometimes the married. If then there is no calling of the faithful from whom the grace of contemplation can be excluded, whoever has his heart

[1] William of Saint-Thierry, *The Golden Epistle* (Cistercian Publications, 1971), XVIII.268, 97.
[2] Gregory the Great, *Homilies on Ezekiel*, II.5.18, 347-48.

> within him can also be illumined by the light of contemplation.... Let no one reckon that he has the gift of the true light as his own, because insofar as he thinks he is superior often another to whom he does not attribute any good gift is richer.[3]

Even when folks have such experiences of "transcendence," "vision," or "union" (what we tend to talk about as "mystical experience"), it's to draw us deeper into loving communion in humility and charity, not to announce that we've crossed any spiritual finish line. It's an embrace of a Lover, not a reward for completing a task. Hopefully this way of framing what's about to follow serves the same purpose as the old warnings not to let less experienced folks read on.

Recall that St. Irenaeus said not only that "the glory of God is a living human," but also that the life of the human person is the "vision of God." Contemplation is the cognitive activity that "beholds" the divine light. That means that the vision of God is the soul's simply beholding the unfathomable divine ground of all reality in contemplation. Who can do this? How can one do this? The reality of what is happening in these moments is not really communicable (though nor is any contemplative experience), but contemplatives throughout the Church's history have "come back to themselves" (*secum*) and tried to convey something of what's happening as they "stammer" about it, to use Gregory the Great's term.[4]

I won't and can't go into a full accounting of the west's approach to these states of divine contact, but here I'll trace out a couple accounts from Gregory the Great that offer some notion of how to approach and understand contemplative states in a Christian context in which the soul catches a glimpse of what Gregory calls the "Uncircumscribed Light." The first grounds us in the basic movement involved and the second more speculatively accounts for the Trinitarian character of that movement.

First, we have the story of St. Benedict's unexpected nocturnal

[3] Gregory the Great, *Homilies on Ezekiel*, II.5.19, 348.

[4] Gregory the Great, *Moral Reflections*, V.XXXVI.66, 364.

vision, which Gregory recounts in his *Life of St. Benedict.* When another abbot comes to visit along with his monks, Benedict sleeps in the upper room of a tower, while the other abbot sleeps in the lower chamber. Then, "When the brothers were still asleep, the man of God, Benedict, got up to watch in prayer before the time for the Night Office. Standing at the window and praying to almighty God in the middle of the night, he suddenly saw a light pour down that routed all the shadows. It shone with such splendor that it surpassed daylight, even though it was shining in the darkness. A wonderful thing followed in this vision, for as Benedict reported later, the whole world was brought before his eyes as if collected in a single ray of sunlight."

Gregory then explains to his partner in the dialogues that shape his book, his deacon Peter, how it would be possible for someone to see the whole world gathered up in a single ray of light.

> To a person who sees the Creator, every creature looks narrow by comparison.... For the capacity of the mind[5] is expanded by the light of interior contemplation. It is so enlarged by God that it becomes greater than the world. Indeed, the soul becomes greater than itself through contemplation. For when the contemplative soul is ravished by the light of God, it is dilated.... When it is said that the whole world was collected before his eyes, this does not mean that heaven and earth were shrunk, but that the soul was expanded. Swept up into God, it can easily see whatever is beneath God.

This is an archetypal experience of divine union or "unitive experience" in the western tradition: it is set in the context of silent prayer; it is not sought but suddenly breaks in on the one praying; the one praying beholds light that is not physical light but spiritual, yet the experience is still somehow related to the everyday world;

[5] Recall that for Gregory and other early writers, "the mind" is the collective name for the cognitive powers of the soul and/or the principle of the soul itself.

that everyday world is somehow transformed in the experience, though not outwardly or objectively but in the soul of the one praying. This, and Gregory's and other early writers' recounting of similar movements of contemplation, shaped much of the early medieval west's notion of what the life of prayer is like, what happens when one gives oneself over to the spiritual life. It feeds the desire to seek "the one thing necessary" (Luke 10:42), as Dame Gertrude More so frequently put it.

But let's meditate on what Gregory says about the experience as well. Two lessons stand out. First, there is the way in which the intuitive vision of the Uncircumscribed Light transforms and influences one's perception of all created reality. In light of this Light, creation seems "narrow" and "beneath." I hope we can see what Gregory means here—our own and all of creation's contingency and limitations compared with God's divine necessity and freedom—but there is also the temptation to see creation as intrinsically insignificant in descriptions like this. If we take these descriptions in the context of what these teachers say in other places about the precious nature of creatures, their beauty, and their support of us on our spiritual path, hopefully we can avoid this diminishment of creatures even as we marvel at what great gifts the Creator offers us. (I'm afraid that not everyone in the long tradition has been able to balance this well.) The second lesson can help us keep the temptation in check, as Gregory notes that creation itself doesn't become small, but rather the soul "dilates," expands. Though he has to use spatial metaphors, he's clearly not talking about a soul getting physically bigger, since a soul isn't physical and doesn't have a size to begin with. Rather the soul's power of vision or understanding is becoming more expansive. One hopes too that as that understanding becomes more expansive, the heart keeps pace. This is the reason, once again, for the warnings about humility and the unexceptional nature of the exceptional in discussions of this most intimate and strange of contemplative experiences.

(A side note: though I say above that Benedict's vision is an archetypal experience in the western tradition, I was delighted to discover a while back that it's more than that too. During a silent retreat at the Jesuit Retreat House on Wisconsin's Lake Winnebago, I was reading St. Gregory Palamas's *Triads*. Gregory was a great defender of Hesychasm in the Eastern tradition, and he had much to say about the divine Light. I was shocked and delighted to read one evening in my cell that as Gregory broached the subject of the divine Light, he referred to a certain monk who had had an encounter with such Light as he was praying once before the Night Office... Anyhow.)

We could leave it there, and I don't actually want to linger too long on this aspect of contemplation, because it can fascinate and appeal to us in ways that aren't always healthy for our spiritual lives. It will come as it comes, if it comes at all. But it is indeed part of those lives if we're given the grace, so it has to be addressed. And I'd also like to push this a bit further for one particular reason: for those of us who are Trinitarian Christians, I think it's important to have a lively and conscious sense of what that Trinitarian belief entails, especially in these most intimate areas of our spiritual lives.

While the dogma of the Trinity can feel completely abstract, for many contemplatives in the Church it has actually been a deep wellspring of spiritual draughts, informing not only what we "think about God," but the way we relate to the divine (our prayer), the way we understand what it means to be made in the "image of God" (our anthropology), and the way we encounter the rest of creation (our manner of living on the earth). Believing God to be a blessed Trinity can undergird and guide our sense of what it means for God to *be* "love" (1 Jn. 4:8), for humans to be images of that self-emptying love, and for the relational nature of all reality—what the modern Benedictine Dom Henri Le Saux (Swami Abhishiktananda) called *being-with* rather than just *being*.[6] And this can all inform our way

[6] Swami Abhishiktananda, *Saccidananda: A Christian Approach to Advaitic Experience* (ISPCK, 1974), 109. "At the very Source of Being...there is *koinonia, co-esse,* 'being-with,' 'being-together,' community of being, mutual love and communication of life, an eternal call to each other, an eternal rest in each

of understanding those brief moments when we touch "the hem of the uncircumscribed light" before returning "with a sigh to the darkness."[7] For those readers who do not profess belief in the Trinity of Persons in the Unity of the divine substance, I hope you can still find some fruit in the following discussion of this oft-neglected aspect of the western contemplative tradition. For those readers who do profess belief in the Trinity, I hope that this contemplative context can awaken a newfound sense of how profoundly the Trinitarian nature of God can shape the spiritual life.

A TRINITARIAN SENSE OF CONTEMPLATION'S "HEIGHTS"

Gregory the Great attempts to say something about the Trinitarian nature of contemplation in his *Moral Reflections on the Book of Job.* In one of the longest stretches in which he discusses contemplation anywhere, Gregory uses Job 4:16 to develop a Trinitarian sense of what it is we "see" from its heights. It's not just that our soul interiorly sees a static unity of all things—though there's that too—but that our souls are taken into a clearer experience of the Trinitarian life of divine relations that sustains all things. Citing other biblical passages in his rumination on this verse (Gen. 1:27, Wis. 7:26, Heb. 1:3), Gregory draws out St. Paul's insight that the Son "is the image of the invisible God" (Col. 1:15):

> So when eternity is perceived, insofar as it is possible for our weak human nature, his image is brought and placed before the eyes of our mind; since we are on the road to the Father, in accordance with our capacity, we see him through his image, that is, through the Son. Through that image that was born of him who is without

---

other. In its most impenetrable core of non-duality Being is threefold movement within Itself towards Itself, the triple achievement of Itself in Itself. Those who trust in intellect will call this myth of wistful abstraction; but Jesus said that only the Son knows and reveals the Father and only the Father knows and reveals the Son to those whom he has chosen."

[7] Gregory the Great, *Homilies on Ezekiel,* II.2.12, 288.

> beginning, we try in some way to discern him who is without beginning and without end. That is why Truth himself has said in the gospel, "No one comes to the Father except through me."[8]

On "the road to the Father," we see the first Person of the Trinity as we catch a glimpse of his image, the second Person of the Trinity, who made himself present with us in his Incarnation and continues to make himself present with us in the sacraments and especially the Eucharist.

But how does that presence remain after the Ascension? Christ tells us that he will send the Paraclete, the Holy Spirit, the third Person of the Trinity, after he ascends to his Father and our Father, and the Holy Spirit coming down on the apostles like tongues of flame spreads the Trinity's grace far and wide through the Church's foundation. And Gregory sees a similar dynamic at work in our own contemplative interaction with the Trinity. Unsurprisingly, he takes Job 4:16's reference to "a voice like the sound of a light breeze" as the Holy Spirit:

> [The Holy Spirit's] enlightenment touches us lightly, but he harshly cuts through our lack of resourcefulness.... [W]hen we are elevated in high contemplation, we touch a slender reality concerning the knowledge of eternity, so we have recourse to the words of sacred history, where the illustrious prophet learned something about the knowledge of God [1 Kings 19:11-12].
>
> We are told that God is neither in the turbulent wind nor in the fire, but his presence in the gentle whispering breeze is not denied. Obviously, for the mind rapt in high contemplation, whatever it manages to see perfectly is not God. But when it sees something subtle, it is what it hears from the incomprehensible nature of eternity. It is as though we hear a gentle whispering wind when we subtly taste the excellence of unlimited truth in a moment's

[8] Gregory the Great, *Moral Reflections on the Book of Job*, V.XXXV.64, 363.

> contemplation. Then, accordingly, what we know about God is true when we perceive that we cannot know anything about him perfectly.[9]

The Holy Spirit brings the "beyond" of the Trinity into contact with our soul's understanding, albeit in ways that make that "unlimited truth" accessible to our limited existence. If we are uncomfortable with this way of thinking about our relationship with the Trinity in this life, we can recall the places in the Scriptures that discuss the Trinity dwelling within us: especially John 14:23 ("Jesus answered and said to him, 'Whoever loves me will keep my word, and my Father will love him, and we will come to him and make our dwelling with him") and 1 Corinthians 3:16 ("Do you not know that you are the temple of God, and that the Spirit of God dwells in you?"), not to mention the Catechism of the Catholic Church, which boldly proclaims, "The ultimate end of the whole divine economy is the entry of God's creatures into the perfect unity of the Blessed Trinity. But even now we are called to be a dwelling for the Most Holy Trinity" (§260).

In line with this long tradition, Blessed Itala Mela, a modern Benedictine oblate, was adamant in her devotion to the indwelling of the Trinity:

> It is right, therefore, to make this august Triad the center of one's interior life.... This is what it means to make *indwelling* the foundation of my interior life: it means offering oneself to the Father with the Son. Loving the Son with the Father means consuming oneself in love, in the blazing flames of the Holy Spirit. Above all, it means loving and loving God alone and all things in him, since God, who is in us, is love. The contemplation of the Trinity, who is not far from us but living and working in us, is a source of light, of holiness, and also of works that cannot fail. [10]

---

[9] Gregory the Great, *Moral Reflections,* V.XXXVI.66, 364-65.

[10] Jacob Riyeff, trans., "Office of Readings," paracletepress.com/blogs/a-note-from-the-author/office-of-readings.

Her long and difficult spiritual journey serves as a witness that the dogma of the Trinity is not (or should not be) a stuffy, intellectual matter for medieval theologians, but the very wellspring of our spiritual lives here and now and always.

But back to Gregory. There is more in this passage of his commentary that we could meditate on. And there are plenty of other contemplatives, like Itala Mela, who have tried to stammer *something* about not only the heights of contemplation but also about how the Trinity calls us into its inner life through contemplation. But I'll leave that to them. I'll instead close on a note about what happens to someone after these kinds of encounters with the Uncircumscribed Light, how it tends to affect the rest of their life. This is a warning too, though one of the sweetest.

ON COMING BACK FROM "THE HEIGHTS": A CONTEMPLATIVE LIFE

In the midst of his other long discourse on the nature of contemplation, Gregory the Great explains how when we are repelled from our glimpse of the Uncircumscribed Light by our own limitations, the effect is like the story of Jacob and the angel. As he prepares to meet his brother Esau, Jacob is left alone in his camp one night. He wrestles with "a man" (who is really an angel, who is really God—it's that kind of story) until dawn. During the fight, Jacob gets the better of the man, who strikes his hip; Jacob holds the man anyhow and asks for a blessing. The man gives him a new name (Israel) and his blessing before departing. "Jacob named the place Peniel, 'because I have seen God face to face...'" (Gen. 32:31).

What on earth does this have to do with contemplation? Well, as Gregory is so good at doing, he interprets the story typologically. Taking Jacob as anyone in contemplation, he says that, like Jacob wrestling with the man, sometimes one in contemplation gets the upper hand (when they "touch the hem" of the Uncircumscribed Light) and sometimes their opponent gets the upper hand (when they fall from that experience due to their limitations). But what is more important is what happens afterward. As Jacob has been injured and limps along, so "when Almighty God is already recognized through yearning and the understanding He withers every carnal desire in us. And we who, as it were, standing once on two feet were seen to seek God and to own the world, after the recognition of the sweetness of God, have one sound foot and limp with the other, because it is needful that the love of this world be weakened and only the love of God grow strong within us.... Then everyone who is lame in one leg is supported on the one foot which is sound, because his earthly desire is sustained with total virtue on the single foot of God's love."[11]

The "world" here is clearly not "the earth and its creatures," but human power structures in which the vices can work to our advantage. In contrast with that world, Gregory calls our attention to how these exceptional experiences of the Uncircumscribed Light transform our lives: when we "come back" to ourselves (*secum*) we are not able to stand in the same way in the world. The sweetness of God's love is too much for us, and we cannot live in the world in the same way, eager for praise, wealth, power, in a word, *mammon*.

Gregory elsewhere acknowledges the "active life" must go on, we can't stay long in the heights of contemplation, but in light of that Light we've seen in our hearts, we also change our way of living, for the world and its pomps can no longer have the same allure or savor. We begin to live for what is Real and present rather than the empty promises of fulfillment and happiness that the world's powers offer, with souls set "on fire with longing for full possession of eternal light, the inheritance of full vision of God."

[11] Gregory the Great, *Homilies on Ezekiel*, II.2.12-13, 288-89.

A NOTE ON MORTIFICATION: SEEING FROM DEATH TO LIFE

In contrast, the fruit of the Spirit is love, joy, peace, patience, kindness, generosity, faithfulness, gentleness, self-control. Against such there is no law. Now those who belong to Christ Jesus have crucified their flesh with its passions and desires. If we live in the Spirit, let us also follow the Spirit.
Gal. 5:23-25

Mortification gets a bad rap these days. That is, if one is even familiar with the term. It's been fairly expunged from the contemporary spiritual vocabulary, though it has been a mainstay of the Christian spiritual tradition from the beginning. Mortification: the deliberate denial of one's natural desires in order to subordinate one's will to the divine will. If we are fallen people with a tendency toward self-centeredness, we must actively refuse that tendency in our daily living if we are to follow where the Spirit leads (cf. Gal. 5:25). This means at least avoiding the occasions of mortal sin (to use the Church's moral language here), but, as we seek a life more open to the Spirit, we find that further restraint on our natural desires fosters just this kind of freedom in the Spirit (2 Cor. 3:17).

Historically, there's plenty of reason to downplay mortification as a spiritual approach. Some Christians down the centuries have been too hard on the natural desires of the body, and there's been a tendency for middle-class morality to colonize Christian "morals," leading to lots of contemporary comments about one's parents or grandparents who "always told us our bodies were bad" or "we shouldn't talk about sex," and about how fasting "doesn't make sense to me" or that "we should do good for our neighbors rather than deny ourselves" (as if this were an either/or proposition). Yet the modern desire to rid ourselves of mortification is a case of throwing the baby out with the bathwater.

A spirituality that tells us that, fundamentally, whatever we want is good without *serious* qualifications is a spirituality that doesn't take the cross seriously, especially in decadent, consumerist societies focused on individualist priorities and satisfactions. This doesn't mean that a spiritual life should be dour or morose—far from it. But disciples of the Way—as the early Jesus followers called themselves (see Acts 9:2)—are called to face the reality we find outside ourselves without overlay from our internal narratives and fantasies. Without flinching, we must also face our own selves: our desires, our shortcomings, and our sins included. We ought to have compassion for ourselves and realize that we cannot transform a life in a day or a week—the spiritual life is a lifetime affair. But the masters of the spiritual life have called us to mortification all the way down the line, and we should attend.

"If anyone wishes to come after me, he must deny himself and take up his cross daily and follow me. For whoever wishes to save his life will lose it, but whoever loses his life for my sake will save it" (Lk. 9:23-24). If we take the time to really look into our own hearts in regular protracted silence, in the contexts of the liturgy and the sacraments, and in relation to the real pain and suffering of others with unflinching honesty, we will see the undue and harmful ways our body+soul is oriented toward ourselves, our desires, our own plans. There's nothing intrinsically wrong with desires and plans. The question we must ask ourselves again and again (and again!) is: how do our desires and plans depend on our subordination of other people (and other creatures generally) to those desires and plans or ignoring them altogether?

To put ourselves first at others' expense, is to fail in charity. These are the places in our lives for mortification—to restrain natural desires in light of an opening of the heart to grace, to caring for others, to emptying the self in imitation of Christ in his Incarnation and Passion: "Therefore, since Christ suffered in the flesh, arm yourselves also with the same attitude (for whoever suffers in the flesh has broken with sin), so as not to spend what remains of one's life in the flesh on human desires, but on the will of God" (1 Pet. 4:1-2). While we might protest that living lives of security, comfort, and sensual satisfaction "doesn't hurt anybody," we must look hard at the ways that perhaps comfortable lives, while not actively or directly harming someone, may habituate us to failing to see others' pain and suffering. In addition, the resources needed to maintain our automobile-, computer-, and electricity-dependent lifestyles are much less innocent than many of us want to admit to.

One modern Benedictine who attempted to discern the root causes as to why we moderns have allowed mortification to fall by the wayside is the monastic historian and French hermit Dom Adalbert de Vogüé. Though Vogüé's book *To Love Fasting* centers, as the title suggests, on the discipline of fasting, his consideration of the history and current state of fasting in the Church as a whole and particularly among monastics can readily be broadened to most ascetic practices. Though he traces out the specific vagaries of the regular fast from ancient times to the twentieth century and notes several sociological and religious factors, the primary context and cause he sees for the modern aversion to fasting and the mortifying impulse generally lies in what he calls "a disincarnate spirituality." While the frenetic approach to work and socialization of the modern capitalist world surely contributes to the dwindling of ascetic practice, de Vogüé isolates "a certain modern spiritualism, which tends to disdain bodily works and to be interested only in states of soul."[1] Getting at precisely

[1] Adalbert de Vogüé, *To Love Fasting: The Monastic Experience* (Petersham, MA: Saint Bede's, 1989), 95-96.

the modern anthropological trouble this book has been trying to pinpoint, de Vogüé says

> Just as it is unhealthy to be content with observances without caring about what goes on inside, so we are deceived by cultivating sentiments not translated into any practice. Pharisaic exteriority has a no less deadly counterpart: pure interiority, combining beautiful states of soul with middle-class comfort. True spirituality is one that is incarnate in acts. The realism of the ancients understood this well. To despise these concrete practices that make the [person] is to separate the soul from the body, to enter into a sort of death, to fall into angelism and illusion.... We can no longer be content with fine sentiments and good works. Between an interior life that ignores the body and exterior action that employs it as a mere tool, we need an incarnate spirituality that makes grace descend into our whole being.[2]

Excusing ourselves on account of the hypocrisy of ascetic acts performed to demonstrate our rigor to others (denounced by Christ in the Sermon on the Mount), we forget his notice to those questioning him about his disciples' lack of fasting that "the days will come when the bridegroom is taken from them, and then they will fast on that day" (Mk. 2:19). Fasting and other mortifying practices actually invite us to reunite our bodies and souls in experience. Like the early monastics, we do not need a theory to see the efficacy of mortification; we need only try it in sincere and loving ways to see how it enlivens us and moves us out from ourselves to others.

This emphasis on the integrating and affirming nature of mortification was pointed out long before the twentieth century. The sixteenth-century French Benedictine abbot Louis of Blois, for one, saw mortification as the foundation of the spiritual life and was careful to ensure his readers did not take this to mean that we should seek

---

[2] De Vogüé, *To Love Fasting*, 96, 104-05.

out suffering and extreme austerities. Rather, "looking upon nothing as his own peculiar property, [the disciple] must utterly strip himself of all things," in everything seeking "God and his honor and will."[3] Abbot Louis teaches that in the spiritual life, as we practice regular denial of self-will; restraining the senses; moderating food, drink, and sleep; resigning the will in patience and charity to accept all that comes one's way as coming from the Lord for our sanctification, we find that "in genuine and entire mortification lies hid true and most joyful life" (5.1). Why? Because "he who is always dying to himself is always beginning a new life in God." I love in particular his image here: "The resigned and mortified soul is like a bunch of grapes, ripe, soft, and sweet; but an unresigned soul is like a cluster unripe, hard, and sour. No more pleasing offering can be made to God than the resignation of our own will, because nothing is more dear to man than his own will and his own freedom."

Dame Gertrude More learned from Abbot Louis that mortification was a primary part of the road to contemplative simplicity and peace. She notes in her spiritual diary, *Confessions of a Lover,* that we don't need to seek out any suffering—this only offers us chances to fail and/or to sow pride. On the other hand, if we say we don't need mortification, she notes that, contenting ourselves with our devotion to God, we will "deceive [ourselves] and nourish pride and self-love within [ourselves] under pretense of spirit."[4] Rather than these options which put too much trust in ourselves, we need to practice resigning the will in patience to what comes our way. She says to God in her spiritual diary:

> For I find that where I seek myself there I am caught, as it were, in a snare. And where I forsake myself, there I become more and more capable of that true liberty of spirit which carrieth the soul above itself and all created things, that it may more perfectly be united to thee. For this is thy will: that by true abnegation in all things both

[3] Louis of Blois, *A Book of Spiritual Instruction,* 2.2.

[4] Dame Gertrude More, *Confessions of a Lover,* Confession 46.

> external and internal and by a total subjection to thee…we should enjoy a certain divine and heavenly peace amidst the crosses, passions, contradictions, and mutabilities which are incident to our life…[5]

I find this image of the "snare" particularly insightful. What looks appealing, what looks pleasing is in fact exactly what binds and limits. If we could only eat more, drink more, sleep more, say that nasty thing about our co-worker more, binge-watch that show more, post about how stupid that other person online is more, then we'd be content! Then we'd have peace, or at least a sense of self-satisfaction. These are all bait in the snare of self-love, hatred, and sin, a missing-the-mark that bends us back upon ourselves in selfishness rather than outward toward others and the God who is Love. Once we're caught, how will we break free? In the regular practice of mortification, we find clear spiritual vision to resist the snares and instead find ourselves uncannily free in "true liberty of spirit." De Vogüé's call to an "incarnate spirituality" free of the "great modern illusion" that finds expression in "disincarnate spirituality" is in this vein.

Contemplation fits hand in glove with the call to healthy, Spirit-seeking mortification, a dying "to sin and living for God in Christ Jesus" (Rom. 6:11). For, in beholding and honoring what really is, simply and without our ideas and narratives unrelentingly mediating reality, contemplation trains us in abandoning our self-centeredness and lays our minds and hearts bare to ourselves. Not only this, but the interruption of our narratives and fantasies of control, power, and pleasure in mortification—facing the painful places where what we want is harmful to others and ourselves and laying down our defenses, seeing them for what they are and sitting with the pain of that reality, not acting on those desires and hoping for something better—opens up space in our hearts for contemplation as we let go

[5] More, *Confessions of a Lover*, Confession 27.

of our mental scripts and images. Mortification supports contemplation; contemplation supports mortification.

This isn't to say it's painless. It's mortification after all. But to die to self-centeredness is to live unto others, to live with others. Facing the reality of the human heart and wanting to live most fully means dying to all the ways—small and large, insidious and heinous—that we dominate others (or just seek to). We must die to ourselves a little every day, every moment, to allow the Spirit to make our hearts expand with faith, hope, and charity.

A NEW *ASCESIS*

Mortification, discipline, self-abnegation: these are a constellation of attitudes, practices, and processes that we can gather together under the term "ascesis" or "asceticism." The Greek term *askesis* meant "to train" like an athlete or a soldier trains. St. Paul used this image when he talked about not shadowboxing but training "so as to win" the race (1 Cor. 9:24-26; though he does not use that particular word here). Various Greek sects had undertaken more and less rigorous ascetic disciplines as part of the philosophical life, and religions throughout the world have their own ascetical traditions.

In the western tradition going back to the Desert Mothers and Fathers, to be an "ascetic" is to make the denial of one's sensual appetites and especially of one's pride and self-centeredness a central and systematic feature of one's whole life. As we've seen in various places throughout this book, restraint of the senses and the imagination are important for contemplation not because the senses or the imagination are bad, but because quieting the soul and beholding reality of whatever sort (personal, creational, divine) is more difficult the more desires, concepts, and images overlay that beholding.

Ascesis is our commitment, our practice, day in and day out, of supporting not only moral rectitude (though surely, done well, it's going to help there too) but also and most importantly contemplative awareness and a contemplative approach to our entire lives. The traditional ascetic disciplines of fasting, vigils, abstaining from meat, celibacy, and *lectio divina* are perennially valuable disciplines. (The ancient but questionable practice of self-flagellation is too delicate a matter for me to want to enter into here, so I won't.) But in our present moment of history, in our societies so shaped by digital technologies, systems, and machines, I propose the need for a new ascesis, whereby we deliberately and explicitly restrain not only the natural desires for food and sleep, or the natural tendency to let the mind wander, but also the natural desires to have something to do and to control our environment as well as the natural (and especially at the moment, cultural) tendencies to ignore the moment-to-moment awareness of our limitations and impending death and to seek activity rather than to behold.

And how do we do this? Plenty of ways, I suppose—this, like all Christian asceticism, is not about adhering to a strict legal code but discerning the Spirit's call to self-possession, humility, and charity in everyday life. But primarily we do this by restraining and limiting our engagement in machine living. By "machine living" I mean a daily life that is intimately and systematically mediated by and oriented toward machines, especially digital machines. I use machines all day too. They are immensely helpful in all kinds of ways. But they also give me a false sense of security. They enable me to be lazy, to isolate myself from my neighbors (not to mention the rest of the world) in ways unimaginable twenty or two-hundred years ago. They, especially through the kinds of climate control possible today in our enclosures like buildings, machine-made clothing, and vehicles, enable me to imagine myself as independent of the animals, plants, and fungi around me and of the soil, water, and air systems that support and sustain my life every minute of every day.

Today, with the help of so many varied machines, I can see the world as being directed toward and consumed with my desires and my perspective in ways that simply were not possible before. It doesn't actually work perfectly, which is why, I suspect, we get *so annoyed* when the WiFi goes out or we can't find a place in Google Maps. But it begets an attitude, a way of confronting the material world and our very selves, that centers the self as isolated and to-be-bowed-to. It centers the human species as isolated and to-be-bowed-to.

Consumerism is the way this individual and species-wide confrontational attitude is shaped and enacted by the economy.

I don't have to forsake my machines (or others' machines) to practice this new ascesis. But I do have to forsake using them *uncritically*. Machines are not neutral tools. They have habits, orientations, and politics built right into them, given that they are made by humans and intended for human use. To use them is to be implicated in ways of living and mass systems that are often difficult to see. To live clearly, knowing one's self as well as possible, we need to throw a little sand in the "frictionless life." And that does not mean taking a "digital sabbath" once in a while or doing a "digital detox" by going to the beach for a few days and leaving your smartphone in the house. Ascesis is not a "recharge" or a "break" so we can get right back to the thing that depletes us so much that we have to take a break from it. It is a deliberate way of living intended to cultivate a spiritual stance, especially since "the world in its present form"—remember that "the world" in the New Testament is not the earth or creation but human systems of power, greed, and oppression—"is passing away" (1 Cor. 7:31).

I see two primary ways of developing our own ascetic practices around digital machines and systems. The first is larger-order decisions that will have cascading effects throughout one's daily habits. For example: buying a flip-phone or a cell phone that does not have internet access instead of a smartphone. (I won't say "not buying a phone" because I don't want to get *too* radical here, but hey…) While you will still be able to call and text others, and take some pictures, you will not have the constant nagging option to look at this and that (and that and that) app, to see what's going on in different social media platforms, to check the news, to look up that thing you forgot earlier. You can still do all those things, but you have to wait until you get to a computer that has internet access, so 1) you have many opportunities to say "no, I don't really *want* to do that" and 2) you will not be shaping most or all of your spare moments around information, data, devices built from strip- or pit-mined materials, algorithmic systems, extractive companies, the next somewhat interesting thing, etc. It's okay to use the bathroom and not do anything else. It's okay to stand silently next to another human in an elevator with nothing to say. It's okay. There are lots more ideas one might take up, from limiting or eliminating social media participation, to not having internet access in the home, to refusing to use "generative" software due to all the labor, ecological, bias, and copyright problems that are built directly into these systems. Get creative, but hold opening up time and space for prayer and beholding as the lodestar for answering the question "why?" (Because people *will* ask.)

Over the years, I have invited my students into these kinds of experiments in creatively resisting or refusing our digitally saturated habits and found them often eager to try new ways of approaching their day-to-day activities. I don't generally frame such invitations around "ascesis," but we talk about the ways that machine-living straitens our vision and ways of living on the earth, our sense of wonder and capacity for spontaneity. Admittedly, some students are immediately suspicious and finish the exercise by observing that this was indeed a "waste of time." But I am generally surprised at how many tell me they are relieved to have a *reason* to question their habits or that they'd been planning to make some significant change anyhow but they didn't know how to take the plunge.

I've invited students to take week-long smartphone breaks (they can use the thing as a *phone* to make calls, but that's it), using accountability partners. They write reflective reports afterward in which they reflect on how difficult it is to ride in elevators with nothing to do but stare at the wall or start making small talk with other passengers, how painful it is eating lunch by themselves without a device to scroll on (why they don't pick up a novel to bring with them is something I've never followed up on), and other social aspects of their lives that have been incessantly buffered by the insulation of the smartphone. But they also note ways that they become aware of their surroundings—noting how many birds they hear now that they don't have their earbuds in between classes, even that hearing the traffic (Marquette is in the middle of Milwaukee on a very busy street) makes their sense of place much more acute. These week-long excursions tend to lay bare some rather uncomfortable habits. The most uncomfortable of all being (to me) that no matter how much they say they enjoy things about their break, they know they'll go right back to their old ways of being now that the week is over. After all, everyone else does it too. Self-awareness at least.

The second way of developing ascetic practice around digital machines and systems is the smaller-order decisions. These won't have cascading impacts on all of living, but they matter in the moment, and not only to you. For example, maybe you do keep a smartphone. But you decide to put it in a drawer from the time the kids get home until after bedtime. (Adapt as necessary if you don't have kids or they've left the house.) This way, while you can utilize the access that smartphones grant, you will be able to focus genuinely and liberally on what your children need practically and affectionately in the moment. Even when you're in different parts of the house or you're out in the yard, you'll be *available* to them when they want your attention in ways that are difficult (at best) to maintain when engaging with digital machines and systems. You might think of something to do with them that wouldn't have come to mind if you were answering more texts as you check the weather app and the news app or your social media site of preference as a notice came up that you have a reply on Facebook. Or whatever.

It can also be moment to moment decisions. Last night, I had nothing to do after about fourteen hours of work, housework, and picking up and dropping off kids. Suddenly, I had ten or fifteen minutes before bedtime routines would start. I felt the desire to get on my laptop and check my work email or Twitter (I won't call it the other thing) clawing at my mind. But I resisted that urge, and went to sit on the front porch during a gorgeous Milwaukee summer twilight instead. My daughter came out and stood next to me, asked if I was okay, and played with my hair for a couple minutes. Then we went back inside. And I would have lost those moments of calm, intimate interaction with the sun, the trees, the air, and my daughter, if I'd gone to the bedroom to check stuff I didn't need to check on a computer. It's not that I can't check things on the computer, but the presence of mind and heart to know when it's best to leave time and space for opportunities and grace—that's the point. The "always on" life, the screen-addled life, diminishes spontaneity and restricts our vision of and interaction with the actual world around us.

I've also invited students to create their own "acts of resistance" to our neoliberal, digital systems, which tend to be more small-scale or one-off kinds of activities. They have been delightful to see. Students dedicate themselves to only listening to music on vinyl when they're at home for a week or to go to restaurants to order and pick up food instead of using a digital delivery platform. Interesting reports come in, focusing on de-skilling and their recognition of how little incidental human contact they tend to have in their more and more "frictionless" lives. (I'll have more to say about this in the penultimate chapter.)

My favorite was a student going home for spring break who proposed to use a paper ticket for boarding. She remembered that feeling of the ticket in the hand from when she was younger flying with her parents and wanted to re-experience that—she rubbed her fingers together in front of herself miming a ticket's presence as she told me about the experiment. The look in her eyes said that this was about more than doing something different or accepting a challenge; this was about bringing back literal and metaphorical texture to her life.

As I said at the outset, though this book is based in the western Christian contemplative tradition, I assume (and hope) that not all its readers will be dedicated Christians. But for a moment I do want to once again speak specifically here to all those dedicated to the Way of Jesus's followers. And that is to say: To ignore the ways digital machines and systems impact our lives, forming our minds, bodies, and hearts, is to say that the Cross does not bear on all of my life. Any tools or systems that permeate and inform daily living have to be up for scrutiny for the disciple of Christ. The Cross does not mean "Convenience is cool as long as I believe the right things." The Cross is a demand that calls *everything* into question.

It is good to be critical as hearts, minds, the earth, and other creatures are all impacted by the onslaught that digital machines and systems have wreaked and are wreaking on us, other creatures, and our common home. I'm not saying smash the machines—well, maybe some of them. But a new ascesis that aims directly at our interaction with digital machines and systems is in large part simply about making machines *supports* for living again rather than one of the main *points* of living, as our culture has tended toward since the Industrial Revolution and especially since the widespread availability of the portable internet.

Life matters. Machines can be helpful for that. Or not. If we never restrain our impulses and desires to use them, we will not be able to see clearly how our use of them shapes our minds, bodies, and hearts, sometimes shaping us for fun, conviviality, clarity, health, and justice and sometimes for selfishness, acquisitiveness, habitual sin, disease, and hardness of heart. Ascesis will train us to discern the difference, not complacent consumption or convenience at all costs.

CONTEMPLATING ANIMALS AND PLANTS AS ENSOULED KIN

I want creation to penetrate you with so much admiration that everywhere, wherever you may be, the least plant may bring to you the clear remembrance of the Creator.
St. Basil the Great, *Hexaemeron* 5

"That's so cool. I'm *holding* a plant's roots right in my hand!" my six-year-old says.

"Yeah, right?" I shoot back. He's been helping me dig and pry baby trees out of the scrappy flower bed in front of our East Village flat in Milwaukee.

"It's like a string down here!" he delights as he slides his fingers down the taproot. "That's why it's so great being a gardener," he teaches me.

"That's why I like it too. You get to know different creatures and the ways they live." I'm fatherly pleased that my invitation to help weed has resulted in these kinds of comments. I'm trying and hoping to get my kids to grow up seeing the creatures around them as living kin here on our common home. Some encouraging signs in the morning sun along a busy-ish street in the deep city. My other son's meltdown about an earwig in his bedroom earlier was less encouraging, but we take what we can get.

While humans' position above the rest of creation is a theme all the way back to the Church Fathers and Scriptures before them, the key in which that theme has found expression in the modern world is particular to a world that has seen unprecedented human power unleashed over other creatures and their habitats. Saying that we humans are the lords of creation looks different before and after the Scientific Revolution, the Enlightenment, global colonialism, the Industrial Revolution, consumerist capitalism, and the digital age. Basically, before all these global movements, we could have the *idea* of being superior to other creatures without the practical power to subjugate millions of animals and plants in cramped, exploitative conditions and to disturb and destroy the habitats of millions of others without many of us even really thinking about it. But over the last few centuries, we've made the move into very real domination, exploitation, and destruction—not simply an ideal way of thinking of ourselves *vis a vis* everyone else on earth.

Modern Christians have spoken about this whole mess as the "dominion model" of creation and its various alternatives. Starting with Lynn White Jr.'s essay "The Historical Roots of Our Ecologic Crisis" from 1968, Christians have suggested new ways of imagining the Genesis story's command to "fill the earth and subdue it" (Gen. 1:28).[1] The most common corrective to the "dominion model" is the "stewardship model," which is certainly an improvement. This view reads humans' task to "till and keep the garden" as the primary instruction rather than the "subduing" part. But this view can very much still tend toward the status quo, since it sees humans more as "middle management" but still very much in control of everything in the Creator's stead. When we already have such broken and exploitative systems, managing them may not be corrective enough.

Another view developed recently is the "kinship model," sketched by Sr. Elizabeth Johnson, Daniel Horan, and others. This view asks us

[1] For a helpful framing of the history of this questioning of the tradition, see the first chapter (and more) of Daniel P. Horan's *All God's Creatures: A Theology of Creation* (Fortress Academic, 2018), 3.

(begs us!) to give our attention to the similarities we have with other creatures, rather than focusing on the differences. The dominion model focused particularly on human reason as a capacity that sets us apart so dramatically that we can think of ourselves as something outside of "nature." But the kinship model sees the cow's lowing for its lost calf and calls to mind a panicked human parent's calling out for their child in the department store aisles, sees the unfolding of a flower bud and calls to mind the gradual unfolding of a human adolescent into their adult stature. We have more in common than we have differences. (By the way, that's because we're all *alive.*)

I've wondered for a long time how to bring together the contemplative dimension of Christianity and the kinship model of creation, and last summer I came to a convergence while reading the Victorines, with a little help from St. Thomas Aquinas and St. Augustine. To cut to the quick: I think we need to bring back souls, lots of souls.

Let me explain. The aphorism from Richard of St. Victor I mentioned early on—"Where love is, there is the eye"—led me down a rabbit hole with other authors of the same monastery, the abbey of St. Victor near Paris. Hugh of St. Victor's treatise "On the Three Days" insists that, far from being solely the soul's internal, transcendent activity, contemplation begins with our intuitive beholding of other creatures: "By the body humankind is connected to the world below, and by the spirit it is lifted up toward God above. It was necessary that the creation of visible things be so arranged that human beings would recognize in them exteriorly what the invisible good they were to seek within is like."[2] And this goes back through the tradition. St. Bonaventure speaks at length about how the "vestiges" of the Creator found in all creatures can help "the observer...rise... to the knowledge of the immense power, wisdom, and goodness of the Creator" as one contemplates them.[3] Much earlier, St. Isidore

[2] Hugh of St. Victor, "On the Three Days" in *Trinity and Creation,* edited by Boyd Taylor Coolman and Dale M. Coulter (Brepols, 2010), 49-102 at 74.
[3] Bonaventure, *The Journey of the Mind to God* (Hackett, 1993), 1.11, 8.

states clearly in his *Sentences* that "From the beauty of the limited creature, God makes known his own beauty that is in no way limited, so that the human being can return to God by these very same vestiges by which he turned away from him, in order that, because he turned himself away from the form of the Creator through love of the beautiful creature, he might return back again through the beauty of the creature to the beauty of the Creator."[4] And we find this too in Gregory the Great, who says "God's whispers to us have as many passages as the works of creation governed by God himself. When we see all that God has created, you see, we are rapt in wonder at the Creator.... When we zealously organize the knowledge of God gathered from the consideration of his creation, we open up, as it were, the passages of his whispers to us.... The things that are public cause that which lies hidden to be revealed in us."[5]

While we can hear these "whispers," see these "vestiges" in creation around us without asserting that other creatures have souls, I wonder how much our abandonment of this notion plays into our ability to give the lion's share of our attention to machines rather than the other creatures we share the planet with. Why we care so much about what's streaming but not about what little animals live in our backyard or what plants are growing down along the river. The separation of ourselves and our activities from other creatures through industrialization and mass media and our obsession with utility, efficiency, and comfort conditions us to miss the importance of those other creatures for our own wellbeing as they become just a bunch of things out there. But what if they were creatures made up of body+soul like us? And not in a sentimental or romantic kind of view, but one that simply recognizes life is still unexplainable in empirical terms and the soul reveals not only what it is to be alive but also how all living things are related in their soulfulness?

Before anyone sounds the heresy alarm, consider that it was assumed among learned Christians (and one assumes the unlearned

[4] Isidore of Seville, *Sententiae* (Newman Press, 2018), 4.2b.
[5] Gregory the Great, *Moral Reflections*, V.XXIX.52.

too, but they were not able to leave us much to go on unfortunately) that animals and plants have souls. To be careful here, the tradition doesn't accord them *eternal* souls or *rational* souls, but souls none the less. Plants (and creatures like them—one would guess fungi, lichen, et al.?) have what Aristotle and then Christian authors called "vegetative souls." These are souls that are occupied with natural growth, nutrition, and reproduction. Animals (and creatures like them—maybe bacteria?) have what Aristotle and then Christian authors called "sensitive souls." These are souls that have the vegetative powers but also have the ability to respond readily to their surroundings and can move on their own according to their desire. The idea was—and this is where the ancient Hebrew conception parallels the pagan—that to be a living creature simply was to have a soul. The soul is the animating principle of an organism. We've got souls, but so does anything we can describe as alive. All these creatures with souls: little muskrat souls and violet souls, clubmoss souls and African elephant souls. So many different kinds of souls!

Fortuitously, one trajectory that twentieth-century Catholic existentialist philosopher, Gabriel Marcel, insisted upon as a path for resisting *technique*-driven civilization was precisely to tend more and more to life:

> For there is no doubt that the technical environment is the poorest possible in life, the furthest possible removed from nature.... So the problem...is only to know how we may struggle efficaciously against the excesses of technocracy.... What I think we need today is to react with our whole strength against that dissociation of life from spirit which a bloodless rationalism has brought about.... Perhaps the most important task on the plane of speculation is to deepen once again the notion of life itself in the light of the highest and most genuine religious thought.[6]

[6] Gabriel Marcel, *The Decline of Wisdom,* 11, 19.

Since, for the earlier tradition, "life" meant "souls," one part of deepening our sense of life again, in resistance to our conditioning by and for machines, is to celebrate the souls of all our living kin.

Aristotle, Augustine, Aquinas, and many lesser luminaries—all were comfortable talking about these souls. Though they found them rather boring, it seems, as they didn't spend much time discussing them and focused their efforts quickly instead on that unique phenomenon, the rational human soul. But precisely here is where the kinship model can intervene. Augustine and crew focused on the *differences* between humans and other living creatures: humans have reason, the others don't, so let's think about how humans are special. And "special" ends up meaning "more important" than everything else, which ends up meaning eventually that everything is a "thing" intended for humans' use. That's a lot of abstract leaps, but it's also the world we've inherited.

Instead, we might focus on the ways that we are *similar* to other creatures: how we all experience pain in one way or another, the ways we also strive to grow and thrive before our souls leave our bodies and the sun sets on our little lives, the ways our memories stay with us and shape us, even when we don't want them to, the ways our bodies inhabit space and time and interact with everything around us even when we don't notice. So many similarities.

If the souls of living creatures could serve as a reminder of our shared precarious lives together, what might the reminder open up to our field of vision? While the early Christian view held that humans were in some way special and set over the rest of creation in a vast drama we call salvation history, in the pre-modern world we were also still *a part of creation* along with other creatures, all moving toward a Creator who made us out of love.

With the Scientific Revolution and the Enlightenment, we see a dramatic shift in the way "nature" and other creatures are described. Though we don't want to lean too much on a couple of regular intellectual punching bags, Francis Bacon's (1561-1626) explicitly articulated view that we are to "establish and extend the power and dominion of the human race itself over the universe,"[7] and Descartes's views that plants and animals do not have souls but are only biological machines,[8] and that human bodies too with all their activities (from digestion up to the imprinting of sense impressions on the imagination) are only biological machines,[9] contributed substantially to a shift in human self-perception which in turn reflected a shift that was happening around these early modern thinkers. No longer a community of creatures working together toward the end of time, humans and other creatures were set into an instrumental relationship of domination. We the masters, everything else our tools for our own advancement.

Souls were not necessary in this picture of "nature" and its masters, humans. A soul became simply the spiritual, thinking thing humans have. And then with the rise of materialism, that went away too. Now for many, if soul has any resonance whatsoever, it is mainly a sentimental way of talking about our deepest held values or the source of our emotions or affections. As we saw in the earlier chapter on the traditional teaching on souls, they're anything but sentimental or abstract. They are the animating force of all living things, what enables us to sense the world around us, what enables intelligent creatures to think, discern, and intuit.

Contemplation, the simple beholding of other creatures, can help to heal our sight. When we shift our attention and affection away from TV and computer screens toward our fellow creatures, we start to understand their lives intuitively. As English author J.R.R. Tolkien describes, this way of knowing other creatures is a "pure (real) science…a spirit coeval with the rational mind," not an instrumental knowledge but one "entirely unconcerned with 'doing' anything with

[7] Francis Bacon, "The New Organon" in *Francis Bacon: A Selection of His Works* (Odyssey Press, 1965), 325-75 at 374.
[8] See Stephen Gaukroger, *Descartes' System of Natural Philosophy* (Cambridge University Press, 2002), chapter 7.
[9] See e.g., René Descartes, "Treatise on Man" in *The Philosophical Writings of Descartes*, vol. 1 (Cambridge University Press, 1985), 99-108, esp. 99 and 108.

the knowledge."[10] I found in my own recent experience how important and enriching Tolkien's non-instrumental knowledge of other creatures is. I've always enjoyed walks away from the world we've built for ourselves, but since the 2020 pandemic have sought these spaces out more and more. At first, I just wanted to get out of the house with my three small kids. But after starting to spend so much time in what in Wisconsin are called the State Natural Areas (600+ sites of the highest preservation status in the state), the creatures I encountered started to teach me about their lives. From a modern human perspective enclosed in walls, pavement, and digital devices, they are hidden lives, especially when we encounter plants, moss, lichen. Thomas Aquinas himself says that "Life in plants is hidden."[11]

They are lives nonetheless, and begin to reveal themselves to attention and care. In one State Natural Area, walking through a pathless summer bog and happening upon a sprawling community of pitcher plants, I was overcome by the lives these little creatures had been living there for millennia. Their lives go on, populating their small bog in the midst of the moraine the Wisconsin glacier left here 15,000 years ago, whether any human ever sets eyes on them or no. To be able to see them, touch them, spend some time with them, is a great gift. And I've had too many such contemplative encounters with plants and other creatures to count or recount.

But one of the most fascinating things about going out into "wild" areas to see what lived there has been how it has trained my eyes, ears, and nose to perceive the plants and animals around me in the city as well. Suddenly whole worlds throughout the city of Milwaukee made themselves known to me, and I began growing more native plants around my home, which at the time lay in a formerly red-lined district with houses practically on top of one another. But so much life can thrive even there in our cluttered city. And when you invite the plants in, you invite the insects in, and the rabbits, and the chipmunks. And suddenly we have a whole ensouled

[10] J.R.R. Tolkien, *The Letters of J.R.R. Tolkien* (Houghton Mifflin, 1981), 192.
[11] Thomas Aquinas, *Summa Theologiae*, I.69.2.ad.1.

community that didn't exist before. I see a thistle growing at the edge of the flower bed, and instead of uprooting it because it's a weed, I leave it because it has a soul and wants to grow, and so do I, and so do my kids. And if I let it grow, I know that the goldfinches will come and sit on its stems and pluck the tiny seeds out of the thistle down. And they did. And it was a delight to watch them and know that I helped these little creatures to continue, to endure, in this small corner of the earth. This is kinship. And it starts with retraining the eye in contemplation. "Where love is, there is the eye."

I've similarly begun inviting my students to turn their eyes toward our kin. I don't begin with conceptualizations and speculations like "Hey, plants have souls," but rather with the simple and practical turning of awareness. In a class on eco-critical perspectives for Honors freshman, all students have what I call a "Natural Phenomena" journal, in which they sit with a given "natural phenomenon" for five or ten minutes each week, write a ten-twelve sentence journal entry about their relationship with that phenomenon, and take a picture to upload with their journal. Entries treat clouds, moss, lichen, wild birds, wild forbs, et al. I explicitly tell them that reflections *about* the things will not receive credit, nor will moralizations of them. (A reflection on how "resilient" lichen is and that's like me etc. etc. is not about a specific organism and its relationship with you but an abstraction that only uses the creature to generate ideas, and that's the opposite of what I'm hoping for in these encounters.)

While students struggle at first with this assignment—they're trained to think about "nature" in the abstract, so I don't blame them—as I continue to push them to simply encounter what's actually there, to attend to the life of this creature (or its role in earth systems or deep geological time in the case of clouds or rocks), their consciousness turns and for the most part I see a dramatic shift in their ability to articulate these relationships over ten weeks. Greater attention to the forms of a plant or the sounds a wild bird on campus makes, the realization that these wild plants are all over campus (in the cracks between sidewalks and buildings, at the back of the landscaped beds, on the ridges on the sides of buildings!), a recognition of a sympathy between the rhythms of their own life and the life of moss found on the asphalt between curb and sidewalk on one of the busiest streets in town—all this starts appearing in week three or four, because they've started re-directing their eyes to life and to the earth rather than to our buildings and our devices.

It's very encouraging to watch. If that is a main takeaway for them from our time together as student and teacher, I can't ask for much more. And those transformations that happen are not due to my informational transmission, but due to their own re-training of the way they look at the world. A look at similarity with a curious mind rather than an ambient subconscious assumption of difference and often irrelevance, however much we talk about how we care about "the environment" (another abstraction).

When we walk among our kin on the earth and see them as ensouled beings, living a life in the world is that much richer. Riding my bike to work, I see the small clusters of wintercress growing along the sidewalk and have a real sense that I have many more neighbors than I used to realize. The sow thistle growing out of the juncture between the sidewalk and the Gesu church building near my office is expressing physically its soul's drive to unfurl and reproduce, and campus is that much more alive and invigorating. We are much less alone than we think.

We live in a time in which we tend to our digital gardens of social media, news sites, notifications, and emails for hours a day. Then we read online stories about how lonely and depressed people are. As much as the online world seems like looking "out there," it is very much a mirror, reflecting ourselves back to ourselves constantly (this was probably the case all along, but with the advent of the "personalized" internet it's very much the design now). When we spend much of our time looking at ourselves in others, we're bound to become lonely. Yet we are much less alone than we think. While we need real face-to-face human relationships, and rich, messy ones at that, we can also have many more encounters with living creatures who matter, who have their own intrinsic value if we would but see. "Look at the birds in the sky" (Mt. 6:26); "Learn from the way the wild flowers grow" (Mt. 6:28). When we see the creatures around us as ensouled, as unique, unrepeatable expressions of the welling spring of life, we have cause to rejoice, we have cause to feel surrounded by family, we have reason not to feel like this life is such a lonely one. Rather, it is a grand, though limited and mortal, festival of growing, nourishing, fruitful, sensing, moving life.

CONTEMPLATING ART

Art, while it is productive in its essence, always supposes a moment of contemplation, and the work of art a melody, that is to say, a sense animating a form.[1]
Jacques Maritain

Let's start with a "choose your own adventure." If you're more interested in rock or hip-hop music etc., read paragraph one. If you're more interested in classical music, read paragraph two.

1. Try to recall a time when a song made everything seem all right. Maybe driving on the interstate, maybe at a concert, maybe in your headphones on a bus watching the city fly by. There's not much of an explanation for it. The beat was just what it needed to be, but you've heard plenty of beats very much like it again and again in different songs. The harmonies were probably based in the same harmonies western music has been using for hundreds (and, at least in foundational ways, thousands) of years. The melody, sung or played, fit all of it just right, even though it used the same seven tones and five semi-tones

[1] Jacques Maritain, "Concerning Poetic Knowledge" in *The Situation of Poetry* (Kraus, 1968), 50.

that practically every other song you've ever heard has used. Something about all of it coming together just so gave you a brief glimpse of freedom, of lightness, of not thinking about the past or future, of being *here* and here being okay despite everything. There's lots of reasons to listen to music, but when this happens, you're contemplating music—beholding it, not thinking about it or using it for some other (perfectly fine) purpose. While it may not be the "point" of listening to music, many of us know these moments as great graces in human life.

2. Try to recall a time when a piece affected you in that way that people call "transporting." A particular movement, a particular run on the violin or the low brass coming in. An ascent that you simply didn't see coming but that for a moment gave you a sense of there being something beautiful in the world beyond all the suffering, the heartache, the very very real problems. Maybe it was at a live performance, maybe it was on classical radio as you sat at work and suddenly didn't care at all what had to get done that afternoon. Chances are, however brilliant the composer you were listening to was, they were using the same twelve tones western music has used down the centuries, that the instrumentation was more or less traditional, that you'd heard an oboe or a trumpet basically do something like that before. But something about the form of that particular sound drew your faculties together, and you were *here* in a way that is uncommon. You were contemplating music, not using it as background to keep you focused or to make work a little more pleasant, not to dance to, nor for any other perfectly legitimate reason. Just beholding. While it may not be the "point" of listening to music, many of us know these moments as great graces in human life.

Whichever paragraph you chose to start with, your adventure ends the same: engaging with an aural, sensual form led you to feel something meaningful that was not strictly tied to a concept or idea.

If the concept or idea involved is part of that experience, great, but the form engaged with is partially or totally what led to the shift in one's experiencing of consciousness, of subjectivity in relation to a world, of Reality. For a little while, anyway. And this is what happens when we are open to and interact with art. The more we cultivate a sense of the various kinds of art and the more we engage with different kinds of art intentionally, really reflecting on how what we feel and understand from that art happened, the more likely we are to have such meaningful aesthetic experiences and the more they tend to affect us and inform (pun intended) our lives in all kinds of ways. And these moments when the form in a work of art holds our attention is what we call "aesthetic contemplation."

I assume that the enjoyment of art—film, painting, music, dance, architecture, literature—is something I don't have to convince anyone to see as valuable. At least, so long as we have a broad definition of those arts. What is not so common as people's engagement with and enjoyment of art is an awareness that when we simply enjoy art, we're engaging not just in aesthetic activity (relating to beauty or, more broadly, enjoyment of form) but also in contemplative activity (relating to simple understanding). The active recollection that we can practice (discussed in a prior chapter) has something in common with the ways that art can draw all our faculties together, gathering our attention's various facets into the here and now even for those who would scoff or look befuddled if one suggested to them that they were "contemplating" when they surrendered themselves to the enjoyment of artworks.

But that is just what such states are: what we call aesthetic contemplation. Contemplating a work of art isn't a stuffy, intellectual exercise but rather a simple beholding of the beauty of a form. And beauty for my purposes here might be materialized in the raucous harmonies of death-metal music as much as the sonorous tones of a violin concerto—and analogous genre differences in the other arts. I'm not trying to say any particular art form is "better" than others, though some may invite contemplation more readily.

While we can argue that many approaches to art—usually the ones we like most—are what art "really is," the aesthetic rests in its own value as a feature of what it is to be human, as part of who we are: makers. Poet and painter David Jones insisted that "It is the intransitivity and gratuitousness in man's art that is the sign of man's uniqueness; not merely that he makes things, nor yet that those things have beauty.... In none of the animalic making is there any evidence of the 'gratuitous, nor is there any evidence of 'sign.' This making is wholly functional, these activities are transitive."[2] In a similar vein, Hans Georg Gadamer speaks of art as a "festival"—celebratory activity that is for all and that leaps out of utilitarian time and purpose: gratuity and meaningfulness.[3] Such an understanding of art offers us a further glimpse into the ways in which we are created in the image and likeness (Gen. 1:26) of the Creator—whose work in creation is gratuitous, not necessary.

These gratuitous and meaningful acts might be beautiful, they might be ugly; they might seek harmony, they might seek discord. They're always trying to invite an audience into consideration of the nature of reality through form, whatever else they might do. And so, these gratuitous and meaningful aspects of the making of artworks, because we are social animals and our making is social, are aspects of the reception of artworks as well.

Whatever an artist might be up to in a work, our contemplation of form invites us out of ourselves, expanding horizons, expanding the heart, if we enter into it with a contemplative attitude. Surely art can box us in even more—if we see "our" art as the "only good" art, if we let it inform us in such a way that it closes us off to other approaches, other peoples, other expressions, then it will narrow our hearts more and more. But the openness of art (its ability to be interpreted in various ways because it does not state its own case

---

[2] David Jones, "Art and Sacrament" in *Epoch and Artist* (Chilmark Press, 1959), 143-79 at 149.

[3] Hans Georg Gadamer, "The Relevance of the Beautiful" in *The Relevance of the Beautiful and Other Essays* (Cambridge University Press, 1986), 3-53.

declaratively) can match our own hearts' openness and invite it into a larger world.

The detached pleasure aroused in one's body+soul by forms perceived as beautiful can help train the heart, for, as the Korean-German Catholic philosopher Byung-Chul Han explains,

> The beautiful object is something over against the subject, something with which the subject develops a *free* relationship. The subject is not free in relation to an object as long as it is either dependent on it, or wants to impose his or her will, purpose, or interests on it, and thus encounters its resistance.... Beauty does not *promote* itself. It does not tempt you to enjoy or to possess it. Rather, it invites you to linger in contemplation. It lets desire as well as interest disappear.[4]

When you heard that song or that movement of a symphony and all was right with the world for a few moments—or when you sat in front of that painting for some reason for half an hour, or when you wandered through that ancient church building at a loss for words—the experience of aesthetic contemplation was one in which the desire to hold onto that form fell away. That's not to say that one can't buy a song file online or a painting from a gallery or even—for some of us—a whole building. We can want them, desire them, demand them, purchase them. But that activity has moved away from the disinterested but pleasurable lingering of contemplation. And "owning" it doesn't automatically produce an aesthetic response anyhow.

Aesthetic contemplation is a particular kind of cognitive relationship with a form, a work. In its enjoyment as well as the falling away of possessive desire, in its recognition of and relishing in gratuity, aesthetic contemplation can train the heart in selfless enrichment, the expansion of the heart that sees reality that much more clearly in its whole and in its parts. It's not a given, not a guarantee,

---

[4] Byung-Chul Han, *Saving Beauty* (Polity Press, 2018), 53, 57.

but it can be a valuable part of a spiritual life, especially because of how fundamental the making and appreciating of artwork is to the kinds of creatures we are, in imitation of the kind of Creator we have.

WHAT WE WERE MADE FOR: THE BEGINNING AND THE END

Sometimes when I start talking about contemplation in small groups or in casual conversations with fellow Christians, I hear the objection that all this contemplative prayer stuff is just for intellectuals or people who are "into" mysticism, etc. And I understand, I think, what they mean.

Given the history of Christianity and western civilization over the last five hundred years—the Reformation, Counter Reformation, Scientific Revolution, global colonialism, Enlightenment, Industrial Revolution, consumer capitalism, digital capitalism—the old way of understanding a person, a person's relationship with other creatures and the Creator, and how all this blossoms in a spiritual life, have had a hard shake. And we find today that living the Way tends to become more about holding certain dogmatic statements to be true and behaving according to a certain moral code. And neither of those are *not* living the Way, to be sure. But, as we saw Dom Cuthbert Butler say toward the beginning of this book, "It was the standard teaching in the Catholic ages down to modern times that contemplation is the natural term of a spiritual life seriously lived, and is a thing to be desired, aspired to, aimed at, and not infrequently attained to by devout souls." Contemplation and, particularly in a spiritual life, a deeper experiencing of union with the divine were simply part of how this human life thing worked. We've lost sight of that over the last five hundred years. A contemplative, spiritual life isn't for "spiritual athletes" or "people who are 'into' mysticism"—it's just what happens when we live attuned to the rhythms of creation, when we recollect ourselves and remain present to the present, when we live attuned to the most profound desires of our expanding hearts. According to the early tradition, it's very literally the beginning and the end.

As to the beginning: in the fourth book of his *Dialogues*, St. Gregory the Great tells a short parable about how contemplation fits into the larger arc of salvation history:

> Take the case of an expectant mother cast into a dungeon where she gives birth to a son. Suppose this boy's mother described to him the sun, the moon, and the stars, the mountains and fields, birds flying in the air and horses running in the fields. Born and raised in the dungeon, knowing only the perpetual darkness around him, he would doubt whether the things he heard his mother describe actually existed, since he had no experience of them.[1]

He uses this story to illustrate our relationship to, first, the original humans, Adam and Eve. They had spoken with the Lord and knew an unfallen world in which there was no barrier between earthly inhabitation and spiritual vision. (They're the mother.) But we live in a fallen world in which sin has blocked our earthly capacity to see clearly in a spiritual way, without grace and effort. (We're the son raised in the dark.) We hear about the divine life, about "heaven" and we think "Nah" or "Sure, sounds good, but in the meantime, let me keep making me and mine more comfortable and we'll get around to this God person when we're dead." Or maybe something a bit more charitable and genuine too. In this view, we have our earth to shape in our own image and God has God's own place to do whatever it is the omnipotent Creator does. We've got our turf and God has God's.

But interestingly, Gregory doesn't end there. Here's a bit more:

[1] Gregory the Great, *Dialogues* (Catholic University of America Press, 1959), 190.

> So it is with men born into the darkness of this earthly exile. They hear about lofty and invisible things, but hesitate to believe in them, because they know only the lowly, visible things of earth into which they were born. It was for this reason that the Creator of the visible and invisible worlds came as the Only-begotten of the Father to redeem the human race and to send the Holy Spirit into our hearts. From Him we were to receive new life in order to believe those truths of which we as yet had no knowledge through experience.

In this understanding, the divine, the Creator of both visible and invisible worlds, sends the Second Person of the Trinity into the world to redeem us and the Third Person of the Trinity into our hearts to draw us into the Trinity's life. Through this grand intervention in the visible world, we're caught back up into the invisible world. But this could just be about the faith that does not see, that hopes and believes and that is all. Holding certain dogmas to be true and striving to live a morally upright life sounds in good keeping with this vision of salvation history.

But there's even a little more to unpacking the parable:

> [A]nyone who is not yet solidly grounded in this faith ought to accept what his elders say, putting his trust in them, *since they have experimental knowledge of the invisible world through the Holy Spirit.* In our story too, it would have been foolish for the little boy to think his mother was telling him lies about the light, merely because he himself knew nothing but the darkness of the dungeon. [Emphasis mine.]

Gregory teaches through this story that we are all like the little boy in the dungeon, in need of light to believe, and, yes, it is Christ in his Incarnation and the divine life shared with us through the Spirit that provides this light. But this is ultimately to return us to an "experimental knowledge" of heavenly realities through the Holy Spirit's grace and gifts poured into our hearts.

This is to return us in a way to the life that Adam and Eve lost for us. Gregory the Great had started Book IV of *The Dialogues* with this description of our current state:

> After Adam, the father of the human race, was driven from the joys of paradise as a result of sin, he entered upon the distress of this dark exile we are now suffering. Driven outside himself by his sinful act, he was no longer able to perceive the joys of heaven which had been the object of his contemplation before. In paradise he habitually enjoyed converse with God and in purity of heart and loftiness of vision mingled with holy, angelic spirits. After falling from that noble state he also lost the inner light which enlightened his mind. Born as we are of his flesh into the darkness of this exile, we hear, of course, that there is a heavenly country, that angels are its citizens, and that the spirits of the just live in company with them; but being carnal men without any experimental knowledge of the invisible, we wonder about the existence of anything we cannot see with our bodily eyes.

The new Adam has made us partakers in the divine nature (2 Pet. 1:4) when our created nature could no longer bridge the gap between our earthly being and God's eternity. But not just in obscurity, but through a "glimpse" of the Uncircumscribed Light as through "slanted windows" as we saw earlier. This is the realignment of our story with God's original story through grace and contemplation, the loving knowledge of our Creator. In this we find that contemplation is meant for everyone, not just the chosen few.

As to the end: the general sense of how all this time and world stuff (but not Reality) ends in the long tradition has been 1) big trouble, 2) Christ coming to the earth again, 3) general resurrection, 4) final judgment, 5) new heavens and new earth, 6) eternity. I'm no theologian or prophet, so I'm not going to try to talk about the end times (what we call "the eschaton" from the Greek). Besides, Christ says, "But of that day and hour, no one knows, neither the angels of heaven, nor the Son, but the Father alone" (Mt. 24:36).

What we can speculate on, however, is what that last item in the list will be like: "Beloved, we are God's children now; what we shall be has not yet been revealed. We do know that when it is revealed we shall be like him, for we shall see him as he is" (1 Jn. 3:2). In thinking about the "active life" (taken not as "people in the world" but rather as the times in which each of us is actively engaged in charitable acts and/or preaching) and the "contemplative life" (when we are in repose contemplating the "divine mysteries"), Gregory the Great turns his eye to the story of Mary and Martha in Luke 10:38-42.

As Christ visits their home in Bethany, Martha serves while Mary sits "beside the Lord at his feet listening to him speak" (10:39). Toward the beginning of this tradition of thinking about the different lives with these two women (taking Martha as representative of the active life and Mary as representative of the contemplative), Gregory says:

> Behold Martha's part is not censured but Mary's is praised. Nor does he say that Mary has chosen a good part but the best, so that Martha's too was shown to be good. But why Mary's is the best is implied when it says: *"Which shall not be taken away from her."* The active life indeed fails with the body. For who will offer bread to the hungry in the Eternal Kingdom where none goes hungry?... Who will bury the dead where none dies? Therefore the active life is taken away with this present age but the contemplative is begun here that it may be perfected in the Heavenly Kingdom, because the fire of love, which begins to glow here, when it has seen Him Whom it loves, will burn the more brightly in His love. So the contemplative life is not taken away, because it is perfected when removed from the light of the present age.[2]

[2] Gregory the Great, *Homilies on Ezekiel*, II.2.9, 286.

All the doing that we are called to do on this side of the grave, this side of the *eschaton,* is good. And contemplation is good. The difference is that, with the advent of the new heavens and new earth (Rev. 21:1), contemplation will go on and on in a great, eternally unfolding vision of charity in the furnace of the divine life as we behold outside of time the One and Three of whom the beloved disciple says, "God is love" (1 Jn. 4:8 and 16).

We are creatures, limited and glorious. Our contemplation in this life of creation, of our own souls, of God, is part of who we are. When we enter into its heart-expanding horizon, through the Spirit and in the Son, we return, however faintly, to Adam and Eve's prelapsarian way of being on the earth, in communion with invisible creation. And we anticipate the end, already glimpsing, however obscurely, the final vision of those "things into which angels longed to look" (1 Pet. 1:12). Contemplation isn't for some, it's for all. It's not only part of how we were made, it is what we were made *for.*

HUMBLING THE CONTEMPLATIVE TRADITION IN OUR PARTICULAR MOMENT

For years as a young wanderer, I worked in natural food stores, sometimes as a cashier, sometimes as a supplements-and-herbs clerk. One evening as I was doing inventory on vitamins, a regular customer and I got to talking about meditation and contemplation—this was one reason I gravitated toward natural food-store work—and it came out that I had just become a Benedictine oblate. The woman's face lit up with recognition, which surprised me, but I quickly discovered that the recognition was not one of delight.

She let me know that she'd just been on retreat at a Benedictine monastery out east for a couple weeks, but sadly all they cared about was business: no meditation, no enlightenment, no perfect peace lasting forever to be found. I tried explaining that monks strive to live by the work of their hands, so sure they'd be concerned for whatever cottage industry they had on the grounds. And that Christian contemplation isn't about having a meditative technique that leads mechanically to enlightenment. It's a way of living that cultivates silence, recollection, gratitude, and in certain moments, yes, opens out into an expansive consciousness of what St. Gregory the Great called "the Uncircumscribed Light." But she wouldn't have it. Those monks just cared about money, and she had wasted her time. She'd also apparently wasted her time on the Transcendental Meditation movement a few years earlier.

As much as modern westerners drawn to contemplative traditions seek contentment and peace, we're also conditioned by a culture and society that demands and expects *control, progress,* and *productivity*. And so, often those seeking the contemplative life also seek to control the progress and results expected: enlightenment, visions, the ridding of those personality traits that we ourselves cannot stand. Et cetera. Hopefully, you haven't fallen into that trap. But maybe you do see yourself in this list. I do, at least sometimes. And while I continue to hold up the Christian contemplative tradition as a wise and humble path, I'm the first to admit that the tradition has elements that can be taken as in accord with the progress-obsessed ways of contemporary western culture, especially when the ideas are removed from a life lived close to the liturgy and others to serve. In practicing and thinking about the western contemplative tradition here in the twenty-first century, it seems that both we and other creatures with whom we share the earth would benefit from a humbler contemplative path. Throughout this book I've been trying to suggest a path that is firmly rooted in the Christian tradition. But, for a moment, let's turn to why that humble path can sometimes be hard to see.

In the twelfth and thirteenth centuries new systematic ways of thinking and theologizing were on the rise. These would lead to the great *summae* of thinkers like St. Thomas Aquinas and Henry of Ghent and, more indirectly, to the modern emphasis on progress, efficiency, and productivity. This new systematic way of thinking took the diffuse, meandering river of contemplative teaching up to that point and channelized it into a canal for efficient transport. We can already see this trend at work when authors like the Carthusian Guigo II, the canon Richard of St. Victor, and the Franciscan friar St. Bonaventure began writing in systematic ways about contemplation. They all, in their various ways, describe the contemplative life as a progression proceeding from more elementary to more advanced stages, usually with a sense of "ascending" or "being lifted up" to "higher" forms. For example, Bonaventure teaches in *The Mind's Journey into God* that contemplation ascends from the "traces" of the divine that we find among creatures, to what we find in our own reason, to the mysteries of the godhead itself. Richard takes a similar tack but with much more fine-grained stages. As we've seen, this "ascent" was certainly present in the earlier, looser treatments of figures like St. John Cassian and St. Gregory the Great, but the new systematic treatments reinforced in their detailed stratification a sense of "progress" in the spiritual life that was more linear than had been stressed before.

These new imaginings took the sense of the heavenly being above the earthly and entrenched it in more subtle ways. But this entrenchment also lays bare the apparent paradoxes present in the Christian contemplative tradition. As we've also seen, though our most intimate form of prayer (contemplation) is an activity in the soul, our bodies are essential to who we are. In part based in how the New Testament describes who we are but also influenced strongly by ancient western contemplative ideals, the tradition has long dwelt upon the inner workings of the soul and neglected the role our bodies play, not to mention all the other creatures with whom we share the earth. Cassian, for example, clearly says that divine contemplation of God is the "one thing necessary," quoting Luke 10:42. And yet, due to the doctrine of creation and the resurrection, there is a value in our bodies and other creatures with which the ancient pagan philosophers generally disagreed. If we look closely at what Cassian says, we find that, while strict contemplation of God alone is the one thing necessary, he also asserts that "the contemplation of God is arrived at in numerous ways. For God is not known only through wondering at his incomprehensible substance...but he is also clearly perceived in the grandeur of the things that he has created." Among other things, he is clearly perceived "when we contemplate with amazement the raindrops, the days and hours of the ages."[1] It is this insistence of the clarity of God's presence in our contemplation of his creatures that I think can help us humbly orient the contemplative tradition for our own time.

[1] John Cassian, *Conferences*, 1.XV, 55.

Likewise, the non-linear experience of contemplative prayer can help, too. Cassian calls the most rarified form of contemplation "fiery prayer": when the mind "is illuminated by an infusion of heavenly light" that "gushes forth as from a most abundant fountain and speaks ineffably to God, producing more in that very brief moment than the self-conscious mind is able to articulate easily or to reflect upon." He also assures us that such fiery prayer does not happen as a result of herculean efforts or as the endpoint of some straightforward process. While sometimes fiery prayer occurs in a silent stunned spirit in rapt prayer, "sometimes, while we have been singing, the verse of some psalm has offered the occasion for fiery prayer." The clearest contemplation of God can occur when contemplating raindrops or a psalm verse as readily as in a rapture out of body consciousness suffused with light. For "Truly, the LORD is waiting to be gracious to you" (Is. 30:18).

In emphasizing these aspects of the contemplative tradition, I'm not looking for a naïve or sentimental appreciation of "Nature," nor wanting to say that any kind of vision of light or loss of body consciousness has no place in real Christian prayer. Far from it. Rather, I'm mining the tradition for a description of a genuine prayer of contemplation that recognizes and glorifies the Creator in our humble beholding of the creatures around us, bodily living and inanimate. And when we start looking for it, it's all over the place. For, as St. Benedict makes clear, and as the bedrock of the Christian tradition flies to again and again for refuge, humility is indeed essential to Christian contemplation. Benedict tells us in chapter seven of his *Rule* that our lives are like Jacob's ladder (Gen. 28:12): "Now the ladder erected is our life on earth, and if we humble our hearts the Lord will raise it to heaven. We may call our body and soul the sides of this ladder."[2] This ladder is not one upon which we climb *from* the body *to* the soul or *from* matter *to* spirit. The body and the soul together form the ladder's sides. And we do indeed "ascend" the ladder in

[2] Benedict of Nursia, *The Rule of St. Benedict*, 7:8-9.

Benedict's image, as is so common in the contemplative tradition. But we only ascend in accord with Christ's teaching that "Whoever exalts himself shall be humbled, and whoever humbles himself shall be exalted" (RB 7.1; Lk. 14:11). We're only "lifted up" when we are willing to humble ourselves in imitation of the One who "emptied himself" of his divine glory for our sakes. When contemplation is cruciform, we can rest assured that we're on the Way (see Acts 9:2).

What does this cruciform contemplation look like? As Cassian says, it cannot be controlled and will come and go between small moments of recollection and rapt glimpses of divine light. But what can we do in our day to simultaneously form our prayer lives to the humble model Christ gave us and to deliberately resist the grasping at control and productivity our society instills in us as intrinsically valuable and that so often alienates us from and harms other creatures?

We can turn our eyes to what our Creator has given to us to behold, to what is so often powerless to stand in the way of human use and extraction. That might be a lyreleaf rockcress blossom growing in an oak savanna, and it might be the ocean waves crashing into the rocky Big Sur coast. Though Richard and Bonaventure teach that contemplation of creatures is one early step from which we must pass on to more internal and spiritual contemplation, I wonder if maybe we ought to privilege contemplation of creatures, not to the exclusion of other forms of contemplation, but as a palliative to our species' monomaniacal self-regard. As we press on living consumer lifestyles on the backs of millions, billions of other creatures, maybe in a spirit of penance and charity, we topple the old contemplative hierarchy and see the various kinds of contemplation not as a hierarchical ascent but as lateral moves, mutually enriching, as all directed from one huge family toward the Father together, not an ascending path that leaves all else behind.

Rather than striving for a vision of divine light or supermundane inner silence (though gratefully accepting them if/when they come), we can *see* the Creator's life in the chickweed blossom at our feet and in the crusty thallus of lichen on a branch as we pass by on the sidewalk. The divine ground of all that exists is there for those with eyes to see. I want to see like that, and I think the great teachers would see the need of this humbling too if they lived in our world instead of theirs.

This humbling of the contemplative tradition is ultimately about how we relate to the Creator's world. If God is Love—in the Trinitarian view, if God is *relational* by nature—and we are created in that nature's image, we are *relational* beings. This is the fundamental difference between Christian contemplation and the ancient world's, as exemplified by, say, Plotinus, whose "Good" was completely and utterly One. We are not pure spirits who need to strip away the body to realize our highest good. We are material relational beings who ought to relate in love to those with whom we are in relationship, even in our most intimate exchanges with our Creator.

Once again, as Richard says in one of the very texts he uses to elaborate the fine hierarchy of stages of contemplation, "Where love is, there is the eye."[3] If our eyes are on ourselves, on corporations' screens, on the walls of our buildings, on the next thing that someone's saying in the digital world, on our stuff, we show the world what it is that we love. Gregory the Great said that contemplation is a loving knowledge and a knowing love. Contemplation is not for our own exaltation but for the cultivating of ever greater charity in imitation of the One who loved us "to the end" (Jn. 13:1).

When we go to engage in contemplative prayer, it is best not to aim for *progress*, for the most "advanced" stage the medieval commentators describe. While we accept whatever the Lord gives us as a chick receives from its mother—including great visions of divine light—it is better to aim for the small, for the meek. Best to turn our gaze to the world our Creator has offered us to live in as a gift. If we train the eye enough, we will train our love in turn.

---

[3] Richard of St. Victor, *Benjamin Minor*, XIII, 65.

CONTEMPLATION AS PARTNER OF RESISTANCE AND REFUSAL

Be vigilant at all times and pray…
Lk. 21:36

In the western philosophical tradition, there is an account of contemplation that says that it is not "for anything." What that's getting at that I agree with is that it doesn't "produce" anything—it's not an activity that makes something useful, like a glove or a fishing hook. That's solid; it means that contemplation by its very nature cannot be commodified or capitalized. But I think this way of defining contemplation also gives some the sense that contemplation is about "navel gazing," that it's an ivory tower intellectual's game or a kind of self-therapeutic narcissism that "spiritual people" do to make themselves feel better. And surely, it can be partner to those modes of living.

And yet contemplation is itself a bare and immediate encounter with Reality as it is, not laid over by our desires and systems of thinking and ordering. Contemplation is a natural cognitive power, as the understanding apprehends reality simply, without discursive thought. It is also, in the Church's tradition, a supernatural grace in contemplative prayer, when the soul beholds the "heavenly mysteries," even something of the divine light itself. And so it can also, and I think rightly, be a partner of resistance and refusal, resistance to the designs that the world has upon us and refusal to allow the world to colonize our bodies and souls without clear remainder.

In St. Anthony of the Desert's day, the world clawed at the person—body+soul—with the allures of empire, a decadent sensualism, and a hypocritical Christianity based in doctrinal conformity but really a cover for secular power. In today's world, it's not so different in some ways, but in others it's a whole new ball game. For we not only have knocking at our door a decadent sensualism, not only the allures of empire, not only a hypocritical Christianity only too ready to bow to secular power and privilege, but a world enticing us to an endless stream of warm baths. Let me explain.

In Simone Weil's important essay on the Greek epic the *Iliad,* she emphasizes the way the poem is all about *force*. In the midst of this she makes an arresting comment on the nature of human life in relation to the ways people suffer in the *Iliad*'s action, using one warrior's violent death in battle as an example. Homer's narrator tells us that the man died, in contrast to his fallen corpse's place in the dirt of the battlefield, "far from warm baths." Weil expands:

> Truly, he was far from warm baths, that hapless man. Nor was he alone. Nearly all of the *Iliad* takes place far from warm baths. Nearly all human life has always taken place far from warm baths.[1]

A big part of the story of the last hundred and fifty years or so has been making human life more about "warm baths" and less about the suffering that has always penetrated and surrounded creaturely life.

It goes without saying that in as much as technological advances can prevent disease and make dangerous tasks much safer, etc., there

[1] Simone Weil, *The* Iliad *or the Poem of Force* (Peter Lang, 2003), 46.

is great good in what modern industrial civilization has done for us. We want more warm baths than we used to have. But the massively profitable and influential corporations of the last hundred+ years have been driving toward a different goal, one in which they call the persistence of Weil's warm baths the "frictionless life." Not only do we seek to avoid some unnecessary suffering; we become entangled in a whole way of living that distances us from stark, clear-sighted, and immediate encounter with the world around us through the colonization and capitalization of as much of human life as possible.

The frictionless life has a deep appeal to the human, body+soul, especially to the ego. And yet, the friction in life tends to be what makes for profound experience, lasting learning, wisdom, compassion. And the disciples of Christ have a particular reason not to cede too much of life's ground to the neoliberal, colonial project that seeks to reduce all of life to production in ever more efficient ways for greater shareholder value. Christ did not come to make life frictionless and comfortable: though his yoke is easy and his burden light, such a yoke comes to us as the Cross.

We do not want to fall prey to an excessive or morbid emphasis on the value of suffering, but the Christian cannot look away from the Cross. Any human who is honest about their existential situation, for that matter, cannot look away from suffering and the looming reality of death. For us all, suffering and limitations endure. The Incarnation did not put an end to suffering or limitations, but transformed them in Christ's voluntary solidarity with his creatures. The Passion is *cum-passio* (suffering with).

We are called to suffer with others as they suffer. The frictionless life is always frictionless for some and not others. A surfeit of food, drink, digital devices, endless streams of information (anything we look at on a screen has been transformed into *information*; it is no longer the real)—these all numb us to others' very real suffering outside the walls of our comfortable and narcissistic digital lives. This is the case too when we read and watch videos about others' suffering, however well intentioned. The digital life is not a new life whole-cloth but the industrial life of comfort and ease taken to a new extreme, one that we can carry with us practically all the time and that it is devilishly difficult to see outside of when we are in it.

Byung-Chul Han tackles the larger picture of our shared digitalization of life in his book *Non-things.* If you'll allow me, I think on this very sensitive subject an extended look at his description of things would be helpful, though somewhat dense. Here are three relevant passages:

> The world consists of things as objects. The word "object" is derived from the Latin verb *obicere,* which means "set against," "throw against" or "oppose." The negativity of resistance is inherent in it. An object is something that turns against me, that opposes and resists me. Digital objects lack the negativity of *obicere.* I do not experience them as resistance. The smartphone is smart because it deprives reality of its character as resistant. Even the smooth surface of the smartphone conveys the sense of a lack of resistance. On its smooth touchscreen, everything seems tame and obliging.... Digital media may be effective at overcoming the resistance of time and space, but it is exactly the *negativity of resistance* that constitutes *experience.* The smart environment of digital non-resistance impoverishes world and experience.[2]

> Every age has a different definition of freedom. In antiquity, freedom meant that you were a free man, not a slave. In modernity, freedom was turned inwards and became the autonomy of the subject. It was freedom in acting. Today, the freedom to act has been reduced to the freedom of choice and consumption.... This freedom at your fingertips turns out to be an illusion. Free choice is in fact *consumer choice.*

> [When we use digital tools and platforms] we feel free, although

[2] Byung-Chul Han, *Non-things* (Polity, 2022), 22, 10, 24.

> we are completely exploited and controlled. In a system that exploits freedom, there is no resistance. Once it coincides with freedom, rule becomes total.

I realize this is a bleak assessment of the digital age we're living through, but I also happen to think it's pretty spot on.[3]

When powerful forces offer us their products and control our freedom to express ourselves, freedom to access information at will, freedom to peer into others' lives (as mediated by their platforms), freedom to choose, it's difficult to see it as a problem. But the outsized earnings of tech company executives compared to average workers as well as the open-pit mining, pollution, and exploitation of workers the computing industry relies upon, at its root, demand that we see our comfort and ease for what they really are. Likewise, as we receive "personalized" media and services, the space of our own autonomy is ever more straitened as our choices are nudged continually (if subtly) and presented within the tech sector's parameters. Freedom becomes what you can do within the limits of the User Agreement. The good news is that life outside the digital domain is, for all its resistance and difficulty, its suffering and limitations, heart-expansively beautiful and joy-sustaining. But it must be encountered starkly in practice for the beauty and joy to present themselves, always somewhat covered and obscured, to our senses and our minds.

I hear plenty of readers saying at this point: "But this is all just the inevitable results of economic and technological progress, and we can't be blamed for what we all do."

We make a false dichotomy: Either we make everything as easy for ourselves as possible all the time and do not resist those who lead us down this smooth, frictionless path, *or* we abandon the goal of relieving people's real suffering to the extent that this is possible for us as a society. This dichotomy conflates the Gospel's invitation to make those who suffer our neighbors and to seek justice for those

[3] For the most thorough treatment I've seen of our situation so far, see Nick Couldry and Ulises Mejias's *The Costs of Connection* and *Data Grab*.

who possess less power than ourselves (counteracting one form of unnecessary pain through person-to-person charity) with the elimination as far as possible of the resistance that the world itself meets us with through the comforts and shiny objects of consumerism, given over to the totalization of production and efficiency, indeed the capitalization of all of life. But friends, we have far more options than these.

In resistance to the dominant mode of life we are presented with today, contemplation is incapable of being commodified. The simple beholding of life, the simple beholding of the raindrops (as St. John Cassian pointed to) or the soul's own inner shape, or the mysterious deifying light dwelling in our hearts, is an act of resistance in relation to the forces that seek to make all of life a smooth ride of consumption, a playful dalliance whose ending we won't think about as we while away the hours staring at other people's digitized attempts to stave off suffering, existential dread of limitations and death, and discomfort.

More than this, contemplation's immediate encountering of Reality as it is instead of how we would misguidedly like it to be—unresistant, completely supple to our desires—trains us to live life accepting it as a gift. To see other people as limited, precious creatures. To see the earth as a glorious source of all life, and one that is suffering at its children's hands. To see ourselves as creatures faced every moment with decisions concerning what we will hand on to eternity in the brief span of time given us. To see our tools as just that—tools—not the ends for which we live. However, to simply *think* like this is not enough. That's just more words, more discursive thinking that convinces us that we're in the right. The words and ideas I listed above *can* be commodified—just look at all the graphic t-shirts, bumper stickers, mugs, etc., with quippy slogans on them that preach to us about all the good things in life. They stand in for the immediate encounter with Reality. They are not the encounter itself. We encounter Reality in contemplation.

Even more, contemplation also leads to the basic human states of wonder on the one hand (when we recognize that the Real exceeds our ability to understand) and rejoicing. To rejoice is to exult in what God has done in making a world at all, in making us able to self-consciously encounter it and reflect on it, on our own finitude, and to see beyond our own finitude in the present moment of recognition. That is, when we recognize intuitively there are limits to what we can see *but we can see that.* Rejoicing is a state that cannot be commodified, cannot be produced, but is simply a flowering of response to the transcendent nature of the limited beings that we are in all our glory and humility. Such rejoicing and wonder open up the heart—to compassion, to levity, hope, charity, largely because we give over our selves to our Creator and to other creatures whom we see clearly to be just as limited and passing yet worthy of respect and love as we are.

The cultivation of contemplation in daily living resists the treatment of our world and ourselves as consumers, as producers, as ourselves commodities. It refuses to reduce who we are to information processors and the creatures around us to objects to be ignored or appropriated for market logics. It expands the heart to see the wondrous excess of the Creator's world, to give thanks for it, to revel in it, and to see that in such gratitude and reveling, there is work to be done to share this great vision with our fellows. It is a calling that goes all the way down.

To hell with neoliberalism's warm baths.

ON THE HEART AND ITS EXPANSION: WE HAVE A CONTEMPLATION REMEDY

In case you haven't surmised it by now, I've long been dissatisfied with the mainstream western, modern narratives about the good life: consumerism, mass media, technological "progress" as wholly benign (and inevitable), maximizing of comfort, obsession with markets, etc. I also learned early on that there were long-standing currents of western society and culture that resisted such ideals and goals—non-conformists all along the way, from Romantics to the Luddites to the Arts and Crafts movement to those who turned to the East to the various incarnations of bohemia and on and on. But it wasn't until around my twentieth year on our blessed earth that my path crossed that of the monastic tradition of the western Church. In that tradition I found the most consistent preservation of the contemplative tradition native to the west, though of course it flows well beyond the monasteries' banks. That tradition doesn't have all the answers, but something about it also began speaking so clearly to me about what it was I was hoping for in life. (And this when I was very much *not* living the kind of life one would imagine the kind of person who devotes much of their young leisure time to reading medieval monastic literature would be living.) Something about the way the Cross, the soul, the heart, the Trinity, the sacraments had been described and passed on down the centuries in the western Christian contemplative tradition both helped me make some sense of life and revealed more mystery in life at once. Strange as it is to admit, among the many thinkers who've left their thoughts and hopes in the written word over the last three millennia, I feel the most at home when reading folks like William of Saint-Thierry, Dame Gertrude More, or St. John Cassian.

For a long time, I've generally said that I don't know why that is. But I don't think that's really true any longer. I'm only entering on middle age now, but I've lived long enough to see the arc of things somewhat more clearly. Unlike the mainstream modern west and even much mainstream Christianity, the western Christian contemplative tradition is radical in its call and its demands about the painful beauty of the world and openness to life and time and eternity, the great joy that awaits those willing to veer off the well-worn track of acquisitiveness and self-centeredness. Yet unlike the countercultures I was familiar with before my early twenties, the western Christian contemplative tradition also affirms the great value of tradition itself, that the wisdom of those who have gone before is necessary, and rejects through discipline the spiritual pitfalls of letting the individual's preferences take precedence on the path. To commune with the great souls of this tradition is to live in a community thousands of years old and to face the present moment with honesty, excitement, and peace simultaneously.

But how do we live as a result of this communion? Hugh of St. Victor writes in "On the Three Days,"

> For what good is it to us if we know in God the height of his majesty, but glean from it nothing useful to us? But notice, when we come back from that interior, secret place of divine contemplation, what will we be able to bring with us? Coming from the region of light, what else except light? For it is fitting and necessary that if we come from the region of light, we carry with us light to put to flight our darkness. And who will be able to know what we were there, if we do not return enlightened? Therefore let what we were there appear; let what we saw there appear. If there we saw power, let us bring back the light of the fear of God. If we saw wisdom there, let us bring back the light of truth. If we saw kindness there,

> let us bring the light of love. Power rouses the sluggish to fear; wisdom illumines those who were blind from the darkness of ignorance; kindness enflames the cold with the warmth of charity.[1]

The contemplative life does not lead to a spiritual aristocracy, being above or beyond the demands of everyday life. In daily disciplining of the body+soul in recollection and contemplation of creatures and our own souls, we are invited ever deeper into the heart of Reality, of the encounter of life—our life—with creation and Creator. As our hearts expand, they make ever more room for the simple, the lowly, the forgotten, the small—a simple life attuned to other life, not all the words and sounds and videos and products our culture hurls at us day and night. Even in our occasionally being "lifted up" and catching a glimpse of the Uncircumscribed Light, that Light is a cruciform one, always emptying the self into others in charity; when we "come back" to the everyday perception of the world, we come back with Christ's self-emptying likeness informing the very substance of who we are (see Phil. 2:7, 1 Jn. 4:8).

Encountering that "light of the world," we are immersed in "the light of life" (Jn. 8:12). "Look toward him and be radiant" (Ps. 34:6).

In a world more and more given to massive, sprawling systems—for understandable reasons—to computation, to grids, to markets, to automation, to mediated connections, in that world we need more *life*. More encounter with other humans in person, more encounter with other species with whom we share this planet, more encounter with our own body+soul to inhabit our planet, our relationships, and our own body+soul more lovingly and more presently than we currently do. Contemplation's attentiveness, contemplation's loving gaze, contemplation's willingness to encounter what is really here rather than our own thoughts (or the internet's or the party's or our friends') about what is really here: these qualities show clearly why and how contemplation is a remedy for what ails us.

[1] Hugh of St. Victor, "On the Three Days," 91.

The deliberate cultivation of contemplation opens up our inner worlds and our outer worlds, and harmonizes them. We have sure guides on the path—spiritual mothers and fathers, siblings who have walked the way before us. We can choose to listen, as St. Benedict says in his Rule, "with the ear of the heart."[2] We can live lives of hope and wonder, of communion and fearlessness. We can live lives that more and more develop an expansive heart. With our Creator's grace and mercy, we can here and now enter into some share of what we were made for and the perfection of which we will enter into on the other side of salvation history: the contemplation of heaven and earth, body+soul.

[2] Benedict of Nursia, *The Rule of St. Benedict,* Prol:1.

APPENDIX: PRAYER OF DAME GERTRUDE MORE

But blessed are you, Lord my God, who have helped us and have been our consolation, who have brought us success in great temptation, who create light from darkness and make truth to shine out clearly in place of errors and falsehood.

Stay with us unto eternity. Instruct and comfort us, make us firm, and let your truth remain with us unto eternity, your good Spirit instruct us, direct us, protect us, and lead us in the way that leads to you.

We are blind of ourselves, and there is no light within us. Live, reign, and shine forth within us, scatter and render as nothing the clouds of darkness and ignorance.

O true and only Sun! We adore you as you rise, we enjoy you as you shine, for we who are insufficient ceaselessly fail. In you and through you may we breathe life, take breath in, and expel it.

Sed benedictus es Domine Deus meus, qui adiuuisti nos, et consolatus es nos, qui ex magna tentatione magnum fecisti prouentum, qui ex tenebris lucem creas, et veritatem ex erroribus et falsitate facis magis clarescere.

Mane nobiscum in aeternum. Instrue, conforta, stabili, veritas tua maneat in aeternum, Spiritus tuus bonus nos instruat, dirigat, protegat, et ducat in via quae ducit ad te.

De nobis caeci sumus, et lux non est in nobis. Viue, regna, et splendesce intra nos, dissipetur et in nihilum redigatur nubes tenebrarum et ignorantiae.

O vere et sole sol! Adoramus te orientem, fruamur lucente, quia deficimus deficientes. In te et per te spiremus, respiremus, et expiremus.

WORKS REFERENCED

Bacon, Francis. "The New Organon." In *Francis Bacon: A Selection of His Works*. New York: Odyssey Press, 1965. 325-75.

Baker, Augustine. *Directions for Contemplation: Book D*. Salzburg: Institut für Anglistik und Amerikanistik, 1999.

Benedict of Nursia. *The Rule of St. Benedict*. Collegeville, MN: Liturgical Press, 1981.

Bonaventure. *The Journey of the Mind to God*. Indianapolis: Hackett, 1993.

Butler, Cuthbert. *Western Mysticism*. London: Grey Arrow, 1960.

Cassiodorus. "On the Soul." In *Institutions of Divine and Secular Learning and On the Soul*. Translated by James W. Halporn. Liverpool: Liverpool University Press, 2004.

Fleming, David L. *Draw Me into Your Friendship: The Spiritual Exercises, a Literal Translation and a Contemporary Reading*. St. Louis: The Institute of Jesuit Sources, 1996.

Gadamer, Hans Georg. *The Relevance of the Beautiful and Other Essays*. New York: Cambridge University Press, 1986.

Gregory the Great. *Dialogues*. Washington, DC: Catholic University of America Press, 1959.

---. *Homilies on the Book of the Prophet Ezekiel*. Etna, CA: Center for Traditionalist Orthodox Studies, 2008.

Guigo II, *Ladder of Monks and Twelve Meditations*. Translated by Edmund Colledge, OSA and James Walsh, SJ. Collegeville, MN: Liturgical Press, 1981.

Han, Byung-Chul. *Non-things*. Translated by Daniel Steuer. Medford, MA: Polity, 2023.

---. *Saving Beauty*. Medford, MA: Polity Press, 2018.

Horan, Daniel P. *All God's Creatures: A Theology of Creation*. New York: Fortress Academic, 2018.

Hugh of St. Victor. "On the Three Days." In *Trinity and Creation*. Edited by Boyd Taylor Coolman and Dale M. Coulter. Turnhout, Belgium: Brepols, 2010. 49-102.

Irenaeus. *Against Heresies*. In *The Ante-Nicene Fathers*. Vol. 1. Edited by Alexander Roberts and James Donaldson. Grand Rapids, MI: William B. Eerdmans, 1967.

Isaac of Stella. "Letter on the Soul." In *Three Treatises on Man: A Cistercian Anthropology*. Edited by Bernard McGinn. Kalamazoo, MI: Cistercian Publications, 1977.

Isidore of Seville. *Sententiae*. New York: Newman Press, 2018.

John Cassian. *The Conferences*. Translated by Boniface Ramsey. New York: Paulist Press, 1997.

Jones, David. *Epoch and Artist*. New York: Chilmark Press, 1959. 143-79.

Leclercq, Dom Jean. *The Love of Learning and the Desire for God*. New York: Fordham University Press, 1982.

Louis of Blois. *A Book of Spiritual Instruction*. Westminster: Newman Press, 1955.

Marcel, Gabriel. *The Decline of Wisdom*. London: Harvill, 1954.

---. *Man against Mass Society*. Chicago: Henry Regnery, 1952.

Maritain, Jacques. "Concerning Poetic Knowledge." In *The Situation of Poetry*. New York: Kraus, 1968.

McCann, Justin. *The Resurrection of the Body*. New York: Macmillan, 1928.

Merton, Thomas. *No Man Is an Island*. New York: Dell, 1960.

More, Dame Gertrude. *Poems and Counsels on Prayer and Contemplation*. Leominster, Herefordshire: Gracewing, 2020.

The New Catholic Encyclopedia. Vol. 6. 2nd ed.

Pieper, Josef. *Happiness and Contemplation.* New York: Pantheon, 1958.

The Philokalia: The Complete Text. Translated by G.E.H. Palmer, Phillip Sherrard, and Kallistos Ware. Vol. 4. London: Faber and Faber, 1995.

Richard of St. Victor. *Twelve Patriarchs, The Mystical Ark, and Book Three of The Trinity.* New York: Paulist Press, 1979.

Rolle, Richard. *The Incendium Amoris of Richard Rolle of Hampole.* Edited by Margaret Deanesly. Manchester, UK: University of Manchester, 1915.

Smaragdus of Saint-Mihiel. *The Crown of Monks.* Collegeville, MN: Cistercian Publications, 2013.

Swami Abhishiktananda. *Saccidananda: A Christian Approach to Advaitic Experience.* Delhi: ISPCK, 1974.

Thomas Aquinas. *Summa Theologiae.* Green Bay, WI: Aquinas Institute, 2012.

Tolkien, J.R.R. *The Letters of J.R.R. Tolkien.* Boston: Houghton Mifflin, 1981.

de Vogüé, Adalbert. *To Love Fasting: The Monastic Experience.* Petersham, MA: Saint Bede's, 1989.

Vonier, Anscar. *The Life of the World to Come.* London: Burns, Oates, and Washbourne, 1932.

Weil, Simone. *The* Iliad *or the Poem of Force: A Critical Edition.* New York: Peter Lang, 2003.

William of Saint-Thierry. *Exposition on the Song of Songs.* Kalamazoo, MI: Cistercian Publications, 1970.

---. *The Golden Epistle.* Spencer, MA: Cistercian Publications, 1971.

---. "The Nature of the Body and the Soul." In *Three Treatises on Man.* Edited by Bernard McGinn. Kalamazoo, MI: Cistercian Publications, 1977. 101-52.

Williams, Rowan. *On Christian Theology.* Oxford: Blackwell, 2000.

ACKNOWLEDGMENTS

Versions of some of these essays appeared in the *New Camaldoli Hermitage* newsletter, *Spirit & Life*, and *Living City* magazine.

ABOUT THE AUTHOR

Jacob Riyeff is a Milwaukee Catholic and a Benedictine oblate with Osage Deanery in Sand Springs, Oklahoma, with interests in interreligious dialogue, eco-spirituality, and world literature. He received a PhD in English literature from the University of Notre Dame, concentrating in medieval literature, and is a teaching associate professor at Marquette University. His first book, *The Old English Rule of St. Benedict,* won the 2019 award for best edition or translation of an Anglo-Saxon text from the International Society for the Study of Early Medieval England, and his essays and poems appear regularly in a variety of journals and magazines. He lives in Milwaukee, WI.

WE ARE
Monkfish Book Publishing

...an independent press publishing spiritual and literary books from a diverse range of perspectives. Genres include memoirs, wisdom literature, fiction, and scholarly works of thought. Monkfish books appeal to the seasoned or novice seeker as well as to the general public looking for reliable sources on spirituality. The readers we had in mind when we began Monkfish in 2002 were devoted spiritual seekers, the type whose passion for the spiritual quest would lead them to read across a dazzling array of traditions: Buddhist, Hindu, Jewish, Christian, Muslim, Native American and more. It has always been our intent to publish works of spiritual authenticity for the general public as well as the specialist and scholar.

Our books are available from booksellers everywhere.

Use this QR code to see recently published books:

Use this one to sign-up for our monthly newsletter:

www.ingramcontent.com/pod-product-compliance
Lightning Source LLC
Jackson TN
JSHW020228121025
91802JS00001B/1

* 9 7 8 1 9 6 6 6 0 8 0 1 1 *